Redesigning the Nursing and Human Resource Partnership

Yupin Aungsuroch · Joko Gunawan · Mary L. Fisher

Redesigning the Nursing and Human Resource Partnership

A Model for the New Normal Era

Yupin Aungsuroch ⓘ
Faculty of Nursing
Chulalongkorn University
Pathumwan, Bangkok, Thailand

Joko Gunawan ⓘ
Faculty of Nursing
Chulalongkorn University
Pathumwan, Bangkok, Thailand

Mary L. Fisher
Indiana University School of Nursing
Indianapolis, IN, USA

College of Nursing
University of Florida
Gainesville, FL, USA

ISBN 978-981-16-5989-8   ISBN 978-981-16-5990-4 (eBook)
https://doi.org/10.1007/978-981-16-5990-4

© The Author(s), under exclusive license to Springer Nature Singapore Pte Ltd. 2022
This work is subject to copyright. All rights are solely and exclusively licensed by the Publisher, whether the whole or part of the material is concerned, specifically the rights of translation, reprinting, reuse of illustrations, recitation, broadcasting, reproduction on microfilms or in any other physical way, and transmission or information storage and retrieval, electronic adaptation, computer software, or by similar or dissimilar methodology now known or hereafter developed.
The use of general descriptive names, registered names, trademarks, service marks, etc. in this publication does not imply, even in the absence of a specific statement, that such names are exempt from the relevant protective laws and regulations and therefore free for general use.
The publisher, the authors and the editors are safe to assume that the advice and information in this book are believed to be true and accurate at the date of publication. Neither the publisher nor the authors or the editors give a warranty, expressed or implied, with respect to the material contained herein or for any errors or omissions that may have been made. The publisher remains neutral with regard to jurisdictional claims in published maps and institutional affiliations.

Cover illustration: © Melisa Hasan

This Palgrave Macmillan imprint is published by the registered company Springer Nature Singapore Pte Ltd.
The registered company address is: 152 Beach Road, #21-01/04 Gateway East, Singapore 189721, Singapore

Acknowledgments

This work was supported by Second Century Fund (C2F), Chulalongkorn University, Thailand, and Faculty of Nursing, Chulalongkorn University, Thailand.

About This Book

There is no doubt that the demand for nurses has been great during or post COVID-19 pandemic. Nurses have become the heroes in the battle of the virus, and their hard works are meant to be appreciated. Yet, burnout, stress, and depression among nurses have become the main issues during the pandemic. Some nurses leave their jobs and profession due to the excessive and under-pressure works. This crisis puts a new focus on human resource management in hospital administration to retain their nurses, but, at the same time, the quality of care should be improved.

This book specifically focuses on the barriers and challenges in the process of competence-based recruitment and selection, training and development, rewards and benefits, performance appraisal, career planning and development, and succession planning of nurses in the hospitals, specifically to face the new normal era. This book also offers recommendations to resolve the barriers and challenges of competence-based human resource management by emphasizing the partnership between nursing and human recourses to influence nurse practice and human resource policy positively.

This book is not only important for nursing faculty, students in administration, human resource students, but also practicing nursing administrators who want to help transform nursing human resource practices, to help retain valuable nurses and to better provide career paths for nurses.

Contents

1 Introduction: The Evolution of Human Resource Management — 1
2 Competence-Based Human Resource Management — 15
3 Recruitment and Selection — 31
4 Training and Development — 49
5 Rewards and Benefits — 61
6 Performance Appraisal — 69
7 Career Planning and Development — 81
8 Succession Planning — 93

Index — 107

About the Authors

Yupin Aungsuroch, Ph.D., RN, is an Associate Professor at the Faculty of Nursing Chulalongkorn University, Thailand. She was a former Dean, Director of the Ph.D. program, and Director of the M.N.S. program in Nursing Administration at the same faculty. Her areas of expertise are related to leadership and management, nursing system, nursing workforce, and the positive practice environment. Scopus ID: 6504821483.

Joko Gunawan, Ph.D., RN, is a Postdoctoral Researcher at the Faculty of Nursing, Chulalongkorn University, Thailand. His areas of expertise are nursing administration and informatics. Scopus ID: 57192718324.

Mary L. Fisher, Ph.D., RN, is a Professor Emeritus, Indiana University School of Nursing, USA, and a Clinical Professor at the College of Nursing, University of Florida, USA. Her areas of expertise are evidence-based practice, nursing administration, high performance work system, strategic human resource management, professional development, organizational change, teacher education, and educational assessment.

Abbreviations

CBHRM	Competence-Based Human Resource Management
COVID-19	Coronavirus Disease 2019
HR	Human Resource
HRM	Human Resource Management
ICU	Intensive Care Unit
PPE	Personal Practice Environment
TQM	Total Quality Management

List of Tables

Table 2.1	Differences between traditional HRM and competence-based HRM	19
Table 2.2	Components of CBHRM practice	23
Table 8.1	Career path of nurse managers in Indonesia	103

CHAPTER 1

Introduction: The Evolution of Human Resource Management

Abstract In this introductory chapter, the authors establish the context by describing the evolution of human resource management (HRM) and by providing an overview of why a partnership between nursing and human resource management in hospital administration is critical. This chapter will also give the reader an overview of individuals who have contributed to the development of the HRM context.

Keywords Human resource management · Nursing · Evolution · Partnership

SIGNIFICANCE OF THE BOOK IDEA

A hospital operates like a small city with the same issues related to the human interactions. With its functions that focus on individual performance that affect patient outcomes, human resource management plays an essential role in ensuring high-quality care is performed by hospital healthcare personnel.

Human resources are the most valuable assets of a hospital. Without human resources, the hospital will not even exist. Human resources in the hospital consist of healthcare resources (physicians, specialists, nurses, pharmacists, dieticians, radiologists, technicians, etc.) and non-healthcare

© The Author(s), under exclusive license to Springer Nature Singapore Pte Ltd. 2022
Y. Aungsuroch et al., *Redesigning the Nursing and Human Resource Partnership*, https://doi.org/10.1007/978-981-16-5990-4_1

resources (accountants, consultants, economists, security, cleaning service, etc.). However, they need to work together in harmony in order to provide high-quality healthcare.

As one of the largest and most valuable resources in the hospital, nurses play a leading role in the transformation of care delivery. An increasing number of elderly and complex care patients require ever increasing expert care that must be coordinated by nurses. Additionally, today, nurses are in the spotlight, playing a vital role in the testing, treatment, and containment of COVID-19 (Gunawan, 2020). Unfortunately, the demand for and supply of nurses in hospitals are imbalanced. A nursing shortage was a big issue even before the COVID-19 pandemic. Additionally, over a year of continuous stress, relentless overtime hours and the risk of infection with COVID-19 has caused many nurses to leave hospital settings in search of better working conditions. Many veteran and retired nurses have been recalled for duty in helping the ailing healthcare system and must be re-acquainted with current practices. No healthcare system in the world was ready to battle this pandemic. Nevertheless, it is our mission to criticize, analyze, and develop the system to better respond to the crisis.

Even before the pandemic, there were significant concerns to be addressed in order to coordinate needed human resources in hospital administration. For instance, the nursing and human resource departments most likely worked independently, which often led to poor alignment between them. This was true across all the human resource (HR) practices, in terms of recruiting and retaining nurses, training and development, compensation and benefits, performance management, and career development (Gunawan et al., 2019, 2020). Another example is that most head nurses calculate the number of nurses in the unit based on the patients' care needs. In contrast, human resource managers calculate the number of nurses based on the budget regardless of the need. In many countries, three nurses may take care of as many as 30–40 patients with a variety of conditions. In Cambodia and Vietnam, there is still a 24-hour shift for nurses, which leads to unsafe care and burnout among nurses (Koy et al., 2020). Other concerns are related to high-turnover rates, the existence of bias and bureaucracy in the recruitment and selection of nurses, the needs of multiple generations of nurses, unclear career paths, seniority issues, and unclear compensation.

These concerns cannot be solved without integration between the nursing and HR departments and the involvement of nurses in each component of human resource management practice that impacts nurses.

However, the integration of both departments and the barriers and challenges need further discussion, specifically in this new normal era, which the authors explain in the next chapters of this book.

Evolution of HRM

The authors describe the evolution of human resource management from the first industrial revolution as the transition from hand production to the machine. This period began in Great Britain from approximately 1760–1840, in which textile industries were dominantly on the rise and using modern production methods (Wrigley, 2018).

Pioneers of Human Resource Management

The original idea of human resources can be traced back to Adam Smith (1723–1790). In 1776, Adam Smith wrote about division of labor in his work, The Wealth of Nations. He proposed using specialization to develop skills, time-saving, and the possibility of using specialized tools. He proposed that jobs should be broken down into simple tasks (Smith, 2010).

Robert Owen (1771–1858) lived in the first industrial revolution and was called the Pioneer of Personnel Management. Owen had the best-known model of the factory in his village at New Lanark in Scotland (Osai et al., 2009). In that era, working conditions in the textile industries were very hazardous. There were long-working hours (six days a week, at least 13 hours per day). Children as young as 5-years old worked under the same conditions as adults. These conditions existed because employees were not considered as important as machines in the shop. Robert Owen was the one who provided the solution to prevent abuses and burnout. The 40-hour week movement and eight-hour day movement, or called a short-time movement, was his innovation as a social movement for working-hour regulation. Robert Owen, in 1817, coined the slogan—8-hours' labor, 8-hours' recreation, and 8-hours' rest, and his work had been credited since the early nineteenth century (Niland, 1968). In 1926, Henry Ford brought Owen's idea in the United States and mandated a five-day or 40-hour week working in his factories, and it was officially set as an American workweek standard by the US Congress (Ward, 2017).

The eight-hour regulation is still used today in almost all working settings, including hospitals. However, it may not be applicable for those who work as software and graphic designers and developers, writers, coders, or other professions who require unregular working hours.

Another pioneer is Charles Babbage (1791–1871), who was considered the Father of the Computer after inventing the first mechanical computer (Hutton, 2002). In 1832, he published a book entitled On the Economic of Machinery and Manufacturers. He extended his work on labor division and pointed out that skilled workers typically spend their time doing their jobs based on their only skills. If the labor process can be divided among several workers, labor costs can be cut, which the only high-skill jobs are assigned to high-cost workers, and lower-skill jobs are assigned to lower-cost workers (Guang-zhen, 2005). His study became beneficial for employers.

Father of Scientific Management—Taylorism

Frederic Winslow Taylor (1857–1915) developed a theory called Scientific Management (Taylorism) to analyze and synthesize workflow (Taylor, 1919). The theory was developed between the 1880s and 1890s in the US steel industries (Fig. 1.1). There are four principles of Taylorism: (1) using the scientific method, rule of thumb, simple habit, and common sense to determine the effective and efficient way to do specific tasks; (2) matching workers to any jobs based on their abilities and motivation, and coaching them to work at maximum level; (3) monitoring and supervising the performance of workers to be effective; (4) allocating the work of managers and workers so the managers can work optimally in planning and training, which allow the workers perform their jobs efficiently (Taylor, 1919).

Although scientific management is not considered human resource management theory, his works contributed a lot to human resource practices, specifically in performance appraisal, matching capability, and in competence-based human resource management, training, and employee productivity. His other works related to analysis and synthesis, logic, efficiency, work ethics, best practice standards, knowledge transfer, empiricism, and transformation (Taylor, 1919), are still used today in engineering and management.

1 INTRODUCTION: THE EVOLUTION OF HUMAN ... 5

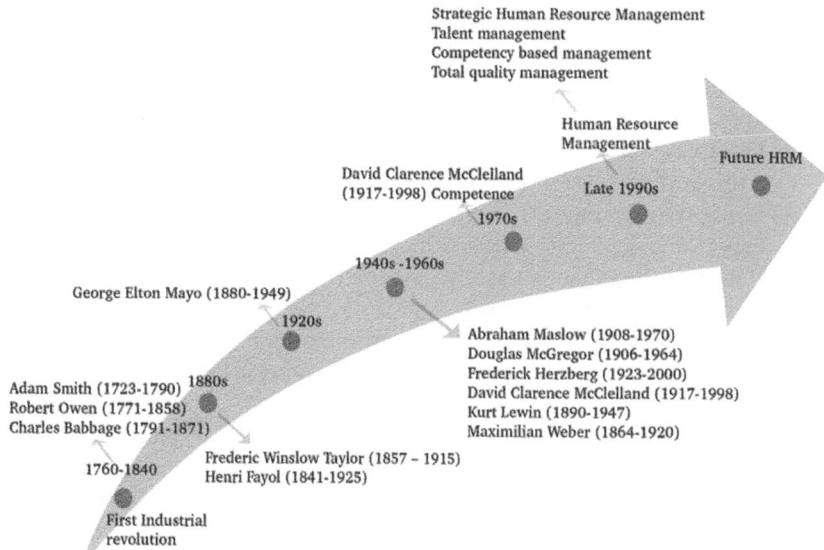

Fig. 1.1 The evolution of human resource management (Developed by the authors)

Founder of Modern Management Method—Fayolism

Henri Fayol (1841–1925), a French mining engineer and executive, developed a general theory of management called Fayolism (Witzel, 2003). He proposed five primary functions of management and fourteen principles of management. The five functions of management in his original work were planning, organizing, commanding, coordinating, and controlling (Steffensen, 2015). Lately, scholars provide other management functions, such as directing, leading, monitoring, and evaluating. Although these management functions are broad, they are still used today.

Fayal's fourteen principles of management (Peaucelle & Guthrie, 2012):

> 1. Division of work—this principle is still used until today, in which we divide employees based on different areas of specialization, skills, and levels (generalist to specialists). The terms "department," "division," "sub-division," "associates," "junior and senior

partner," and other terms have been created to increase professionalism and productivity, as well as to infer a career path.
2. Authority and Responsibility. Gives the power for management to give orders to subordinates.
3. Discipline. It has become the core value of each employee to reach a mission and vision of an organization.
4. Unity of command. Each employee receives orders from one superior in each department or each level.
5. Unity of direction is usually described in the mission and vision of an organization.
6. Subordination of individual to the general interest. This principle describes that the organization's interest come first while the employees' interest is secondary.
7. Remuneration. Each employee should be paid based on their performance and standard of living.
8. Centralization and Decentralization. This refers to a systematic delegation of authority in an organization that is either vertical or horizontal in structure.
9. Scalar chain. This refers to the line of authority from top to low level of management. It can also be described as a vertical line of the order. For example, the line between Top manager and middle manager, between the middle manager and first-line manager, and between the first-line manager and employees.
10. Order. A systematic arrangement of people, machines, and material.
11. Equity. Each employee must be equally treated.
12. Stability of tenure of personnel. An organization must have an optimal turnover rate.
13. Initiative. Each employee should be allowed to take charge or initiate things within their scope independently and be responsible for their outcomes.
14. Esprit de corps. A shared spirit among group members will create unity and enthusiasm within the organization.

Although Fayolism is not considered human resource management theory, his principles and functions of management have been a part of the human resource management theory today.

Father of Human Relation Movement

In the late 1920s, George Elton Mayo (1880–1949) developed his theory based on his studies at Western Electric's Hawthorne plant, which we call the "Hawthorne effect" (Muldoon, 2012). It refers to the improvement in employees' performance and productivity if they think they are being observed or studied. His study's results provided the new knowledge that economic factors, monetary incentives are less effective than social needs or desires to belong in a group (King, 2016). He also acknowledged that social and psychological factors were related to worker productivity and output (King, 2016). Thus, managers should be aware that social and psychological needs and being involved in a working group are important factors than the other factors. Mayo's theory is not considered human resource management theory, but it provides the best input in human resource practices.

Motivation Theories

Over time, motivation theories were also developed before human resource management theory was addressed, such as Maslow's hierarchy of needs, McGregor Theory X & Y, Herzberg's motivation-hygiene theory, and McClelland's need theory.

Maslow's hierarchy of needs—This theory was proposed by Abraham Maslow (1908–1970) in his paper "A Theory of Human Motivation" in Psychological Review in 1943 (Maslow, 1943). He created a hierarchy of needs as factors of human motivation, which include (1) physiological needs, (2) safety needs, (3) social belonging, (4) self-esteem, and (5) self-actualization. He believed that each need must be satisfied within the individuals themselves for motivation to arise at the next stage. Self-actualization is the goal of this theory (McEwen & Wills, 2014).

Theory X & Y—This theory was proposed by Douglas McGregor (1906–1964) while he was working at the MIT Sloan School of Management in the 1950s, and was further developed in the 1960s (Manglik, 2020). Theory X highlights the role of external rewards, penalties, and supervision. Theory X was designed based on the assumption that the employees were lazy, less intelligent, and avoided responsibility, requiring rewards and punishments. Theory Y explains job satisfaction's role to motivate employees without direct supervision (Morse & Lorsch, 1970). Theory Y was developed based on the assumption that the employees enjoyed their jobs and are internally-motivated without requiring a direct reward in return. Thus, they do not need direct supervision. However, in practice, both Theory X and Y are applied simultaneously by the managers because each human is unique and differently motivated (Morse & Lorsch, 1970).

Motivation-hygiene theory—This theory was proposed by Frederick Herzberg (1923–2000) in his publication "One more time, how do you motivate employees?" in 1968 in *Harvard Business Review* (Herzberg, 1968). He stated that hygiene factors do not give positive satisfaction or lead to higher motivation, but their absence causes employee dissatisfaction. These factors include company policy, salary, status, job security, interpersonal relationships, work conditions, incentive, paid insurance, vacations, and other extrinsic factors (Dartey-Baah & Amoako, 2011). The motivational factors do not lower motivation but can increase motivation. The factors include recognition, achievement, competition, personal enrichment, responsibility, involvement in decision-making, sense of importance, personal growth, positive satisfaction, and other intrinsic factors (Dartey-Baah & Amoako, 2011).

Need theory—This theory was developed by David Clarence McClelland (1917–1998), commonly referred to as the "need for achievement" or n-achievement theory. In this theory, he focuses on the need for achievement (N-Ach—the desire to excel concerning a set of standards); the need for affiliation (N-Aff—the desire for personal relationship); and the need for power (N-Pow—the desire to be influential) (Moran et al., 2013), which drive, direct, and select the behaviors of the individual. These three factors are related to each other (McClelland, 1987).

Social Psychology and Modern Western Society

The other areas of development related to human resources are social psychology and modern western society. Kurt Lewin (1890–1947) is well known as the founder of social psychology. His works are often characterized in terms of leadership styles, such as authoritarian, democratic, and laissez-faire. Lewin is also famous for his 3-stage model of change, including unfreezing, changing, and refreezing (Tang, 2019). Other works are related to group dynamics and Lewin's equation, $B = f(P, E)$, which behavior is a function of the person in their environment (Sansone et al., 2003).

Maximilian Karl Emil Weber (1864–1920) is a critical theorist in modern Western society development (Caves, 2005). Regarding human resources, he developed the theory of bureaucracy called the Rational-Legal Model. He noted that bureaucracy should be based on general principles precisely defined and organized across-the-board competencies of the various offices, underpinned by rules, laws, or administrative regulations (Waters, 2015). Therefore, recruitment should be based on merit, a career with a systematic salary structure, a job-scope based on specialization, a hierarchy of power, rules, and discipline (Waters, 2015).

Founder of the Modern Competency Movement

David Clarence McClelland (1917–1998) is called the founder of the Modern Competency movement. He is the 15th most cited psychologist of the twentieth century for his paper in 1973 entitled Testing for Competence Rather than Intelligence (McClelland, 1973). In his article, he argued that measuring competence is much more valid than aptitude and intelligence tests. He also highlighted the importance of personality or traits, which can be changed, trained, and developed. In his works, he also emphasized that job description is no longer valid for measuring competence because competence is identified by what superior performers do (benchmarks) (McClelland, 1973).

Human Resource Management

Although there was no individual expressly stated as a founder of human resource theory, human resource was discussed in the works of Adam Smith (1723–1790), Robert Owen (1771–1858), and Charles Babbage (1791–1871). Human resources emerged as a specific field in the late nineteenth century and was influenced by Taylorism, Fayolism, Elton Mayo, Abraham Maslow (1908–1970), Kurt Lewin (1890–1947), Max Weber (1864–1920), Frederick Herzberg (1923–2000), and David McClelland (1917–1998), as we explained above.

Human resource management (HRM) is the strategic approach to manage people and staff policies and practice in an organization, including the process of recruitment, selection, training and development, performance appraisal, and rewards and benefits, to ensure that the organization can achieve success through people (Gunawan et al., 2019, 2020). There are many models of HRM today.

Strategic human resource management—Strategic human resource management is attracting, developing, rewarding, and retaining employees for the benefit of the employee and the organization. It is noted that HR departments that use this approach interact with other departments within an organization (rather than work independently) to create strategies that align with each department's and the organization's objectives (Bliss, 2006).

Talent management—Talent management is a business strategy and an organization's commitment to hire, manage, develop, and retain the topmost talented employees to ensure the highest performance of an organization (Hughes & Rog, 2008).

Total quality management—Total quality management (TQM) is not one of the HR models, but it is one of the systems approaches often used for business strategy that may include the HR department. TQM brings primary elements, such as focusing on the customer, involving employees, continual improvement, systems integration, process-centered practices, strategic and systematic approach, communication, and decision-making based on fact (Inmon & Linstedt, 2014).

Competence-based human resource management—Competence-based human resource management is the integration of the competence model and human resources planning with business planning to achieve the organization's vision, mission, and business goals (Gunawan et al., 2019, 2020). All HR practices should be based on competence analyses. This model will be explained thoroughly in the next chapter.

Future of human resource management—The next question is: What will be the future emphasis of HRM? Advanced technology, small and big start-up companies provide a lens to the future of human resource management. Agile HR is the right and flexible approach, which will create the HR organization of tomorrow in the new normal era. Agile HR is defined as an HR operational strategy to minimize waste and optimize the flow of value to its customers by organizing the HR function in multidisciplinary teams, which continuously align with changing business needs by sensing and adapting through open communication while operating in short cycles (McMackin & Heffernan, 2020). Agile principles are reflected in all aspects of the HR operation, including structures, processes, roles, tools, skills, and behaviors of HR management and employees (McMackin & Heffernan, 2020).

Conclusion

Human resource management's evolution has changed over time, from poor working conditions where people were abused to the modern environment where people are seen as essential assets to businesses and organizations. Human resource management should adapt to the times as people and the environment change. There are no more strict job descriptions. We may see flexible human resource practices in the future, and the employers may see people based on their values to contribute rather than their cost. Skills first, cost second.

References

Bliss, W. (2006). *Essentials of strategy*. Harvard Business Press.
Caves, R. W. (2005). *Encyclopedia of the city*. Taylor & Francis.
Dartey-Baah, K., & Amoako, G. K. (2011). Application of Frederick Herzberg's two-factor theory in assessing and understanding employee motivation at work: A Ghanaian perspective. *European Journal of Business and Management, 3*(9), 1–8.
Guang-zhen, S. (2005). *Readings in the economics of the division of labor: The classical tradition* (Vol. 2). World Scientific.
Gunawan, J. (2020). COVID-19: Praise is welcome, but nurses deserve a pay rise. *Belitung Nursing Journal, 6*(5), 150–151. https://doi.org/10.33546/bnj.1217.
Gunawan, J., Aungsuroch, Y., & Fisher, M. L. (2019). Competence-based human resource management in nursing: A literature review. *Nursing Forum, 54*(1), 91–101. https://doi.org/10.1111/nuf.12302.
Gunawan, J., Aungsuroch, Y., Fisher, M. L., McDaniel, A. M., & Marzilli, C. (2020). Managerial competence of first-line nurse managers in public hospitals in Indonesia. *Journal of Multidisciplinary Healthcare, 13*, 1017. https://doi.org/10.2147/JMDH.S269150.
Herzberg, F. (1968). *One more time: How do you motivate employees*. Harvard Business Review.
Hughes, J. C., & Rog, E. (2008). Talent management: A strategy for improving employee recruitment, retention and engagement within hospitality organizations. *International Journal of Contemporary Hospitality Management, 20*(7), 743–757. https://doi.org/10.1108/09596110810899086.
Hutton, D. M. (2002). The difference engine: Charles Babbage and the Quest to build the first computer. *Kybernetes, 31*(6). https://doi.org/10.1108/k.2002.06731fae.009.

Inmon, W. H., & Linstedt, D. (2014). *Data architecture: A primer for the data scientist: Big data, data warehouse and data vault*. Morgan Kaufmann.

King, D. (2016). Human relations movement/Mayo. In *Encyclopedia of human resource management*. Edward Elgar.

Koy, V., Yunibhand, J., & Turale, S. (2020). "It is really so exhausting": Exploring intensive care nurses' perceptions of 24-hour long shifts. *Journal of Clinical Nursing, 29*(17–18), 3506–3515. https://doi.org/10.1111/jocn.15389.

Manglik, R. (2020). *UGC NET sociology: 2020| 20 full-length mock test (Paper I & II)*. EduGorilla.

Maslow, A. (1943). A theory of human motivation. *Psychological Review, 50*(4), 370–396.

McClelland, D. C. (1973). Testing for competence rather than for "intelligence." *American Psychologist, 28*(1), 1.

McClelland, D. C. (1987). *Human motivation*. University of Cambridge.

McEwen, M., & Wills, E. M. (2014). *Theoretical basis for nursing*. Lippincott Williams & Wilkins.

McMackin, J., & Heffernan, M. (2020). Agile for HR: Fine in practice, but will it work in theory? *Human Resource Management Review*, 100791. https://doi.org/10.1016/j.hrmr.2020.100791.

Moran, B. B., Stueart, R. D., & Morner, C. J. (2013). *Library and information center management*. Libraries Unlimited.

Morse, J. J., & Lorsch, J. W. (1970). Beyond theory Y. *Harvard Business Review*, 61–68.

Muldoon, J. (2012). The Hawthorne legacy: A reassessment of the impact of the Hawthorne studies on management scholarship. *Journal of Management History, 18*(1). https://doi.org/10.1108/17511341211188682.

Niland, J. (1968). The birth of the movement for an eight hour working day in New South Wales. *Australian Journal of Politics & History, 14*(1), 75–87. https://doi.org/10.1111/j.1467-8497.1968.tb00613.x.

Osai, O. J., Eleanya, L. U. M., Orukwowu, J. M., & Okene, N. V. C. (2009). Jethro as the patriarch of administration and management: An analysis of his works. *Journal of Social Sciences, 18*(3), 157–162. https://doi.org/10.1080/09718923.2009.11892677.

Peaucelle, J. L., & Guthrie, C. (2012). The private life of Henri Fayol and his motivation to build a management science. *Journal of Management History, 18*(4), 460–487. https://doi.org/10.1108/17511341211258774.

Sansone, C., Morf, C. C., & Panter, A. T. (2003). *The Sage handbook of methods in social psychology*. Sage.

Smith, A. (2010). *The Wealth of Nations: An inquiry into the nature and causes of the Wealth of Nations*. Harriman House Limited.

Steffensen, B. (2015). Fayol (1916): Administration industrielle et générale, prévoyance, organisation, commandement, coordination, contrôle. *Schlüsselwerke der Organisationsforschung*, 264–267.
Tang, K. N. (2019). Change management. In *Leadership and change management* (pp. 47–55). Springer.
Taylor, F. W. (1919). *The principles of scientific management*. Harper & Brothers.
Ward, M. (2017). *A brief history of the 8-hour workday, which changed how Americans work*. Retrieved from https://www.cnbc.com/2017/05/03/how-the-8-hour-workday-changed-how-americans-work.html.
Waters, T. (2015). *Weber's rationalism and modern society: New translations on politics, bureaucracy, and social stratification*. Springer.
Witzel, M. (2003). *Fifty key figures in management*. Routledge.
Wrigley, E. A. (2018). Reconsidering the industrial revolution: England and Wales. *Journal of Interdisciplinary History*, 49(1), 9–42. https://doi.org/10.1162/jinh_a_01230.

CHAPTER 2

Competence-Based Human Resource Management

Abstract To enhance the partnership between nursing and human resource, nurses should understand the concept of human resource management (HRM) and its application. The authors emphasize the use of competence in HRM implementation to treat employees equally, matching jobs with their competence. In this chapter, the authors provide an overview of competence, human resource management (HRM), and competence-based human resource management (CBHRM). This chapter also provides the reader with CBHRM system schemes, models, systems (structure, process, and outcome), and components of CBHRM practices.

Keywords Competence · Human resource management · Nursing

OVERVIEW OF COMPETENCE

The concept of competence is developed by McClelland (1973), Boyatzis (1982), Spencer and Spencer (1993), and Rankin (2002). Many others in the field have widely used this concept, not only in business and management literature, but also in social science, health science, and all related areas. We acknowledge their groundbreaking works to develop the competence of human resources in every organization.

© The Author(s), under exclusive license to Springer Nature Singapore Pte Ltd. 2022
Y. Aungsuroch et al., *Redesigning the Nursing and Human Resource Partnership*, https://doi.org/10.1007/978-981-16-5990-4_2

In the literature, the term competence, competency, competencies, and core competencies are used interchangeably. In this chapter, we only use the term "competence" to describe competence and competency for the sake of consistency. But competencies and core competencies are different. According to Richard (1982), *competence* consists of tasks to do and skills to strategically do the jobs. Hroník (2007) and KrontorÁD and Trčka (2005) define *competence* as a combination of knowledge, skills, abilities, experience, characteristics, and behaviors of an employee in performing his/her work. Ellis (1988) concluded that *competence* refers to the attitudes, attributes, characteristics, values, and capacities of individuals, which are observed as measurable behaviors. Ellis' definition is similar to the definition of competence in previous studies as described by (Gunawan & Aungsuroch, 2017; Gunawan et al., 2019; McClelland & Boyatzis, 1982; Spencer & Spencer, 2008). McConnell (2001) describes competence and competency differently. *Competence* refers to individuals' capacity to perform their responsibilities, while *competency* refers to the individual's actual performance. However, Rankin (2002), Armstrong (2010) emphasize that competence provides universal understanding to describe performance in multiple settings.

In conclusion, the concept of competence has been described from multiple perspectives, dependent on the beholders' eye (Dubois & Rothwell, 2004). We then summarize the meaning of competence or competency as:

1. A combination of skill, knowledge, abilities, attitude, and behaviors in performing the job.
2. The ability or capacity of an individual to carry out job responsibilities.
3. The behavior of an individual as the reflection of their knowledge, skills, attitudes, characteristics, and personalities.

However, these three points are different from the definition of competencies, core competencies, performance, and function. *Competencies* are the plural of competency, which describe specific areas of expertise or skill, and tasks to perform in a job (Titus, 1994). *Core competencies* are defined as the required or main set of skills, attributes, and behavior for all staff in a particular role (United Nations, 2010). *Performance* is the execution of an action (Merriam-Webster, 2020). *Function* is the action for which a thing exists or for which a person or thing is specially fitted or used (Merriam-Webster, 2020).

Overview of Human Resource Management

Human resource management (HRM) theory was originated virtually when the Harvard Analytic Framework was introduced by the Harvard School in 1980 (Weerasooriya, 2008). HRM theory was developed based on the industrial revolutions and was influenced by many models and related theories, as described in Chapter 1.

HRM focuses on all aspects of people management and covers many theories and concepts, such as human capital management, talent management, knowledge management, strategic HRM, learning and development, competence-based HRM, and others (Armstrong, 2010). HRM has also been discussed widely with various explanations. According to Business Dictionary (2020), HRM refers to the process of hiring employees, doing job analyses, rewarding and developing employees, and monitoring all employees so that they become more valuable to the organization.

Dessler (2011) defines HRM as the process of acquiring, training, evaluating, and compensating employees, which is also similar to Anyangwe (2017) who described HRM as the process of recruitment and selection, direction, training, coaching, and talent management. Armstrong (2010) added that HRM emphasizes more on motivation, acquisition, and organization of human resources. Quansah (2013) defines HRM as an integrated approach to strategically developing the well-being of the employee. Som (2008) described HRM as a carefully designed system to improve performance and organizational effectiveness.

In summary, HRM can be defined and described in multi-perspective ways, reflecting different philosophies and approaches among managers and researchers. However, HRM is a system generally meant to be applied to hire, manage, direct, and develop employees to be productive and competitive to achieve the organization's vision and mission. Importantly, HRM stresses the importance of job analysis as an HR planning strategy to gain competitive advantage (Dessler, 2006).

Example HRM Models (Harvard and Matching Model)

Harvard model—this model was first suggested by Beer et al. (1984) at Harvard University, which then was called the "Harvard Framework" model (Boxall, 1992). The Harvard model consists of 6 components—situational factors, stakeholder groups and interest, HR strategies, HR outcomes, long-term consequences, and feedback. In this model, the situational factors (business strategy, workforce type, labor market, culture, laws and social values, unions, management philosophy, and task technology) influence the stakeholders' interests, employees' interests, and government and labor unions. However, both stakeholders and situational factors influence HR strategies.

The HR strategies in this model include rewards systems, employee influence, work systems, and human resource flow, which will impact HR outcomes (cost, competence, congruence, and commitment). Consequently, it will affect social well-being, organizational effectiveness, and individual well-being. However, each outcome or consequence will be re-evaluated based on the situational factors and stakeholders' interests. This model is quite flexible and aligned with personnel policies and competitive strategy as long as the organization's goals can be achieved (Anyangwe, 2017).

Interestingly, this model recognizes each stakeholder group's equal roles among government, employees, and trade groups. Also, this model is considered an ideal model to track how a change in HRM policies and strategies affect HR outcomes. However, taking multiple stakeholders' interests is the challenging part of this model. Not all groups have commonality. Thus, it requires competent HR managers to unify all perspectives and interests.

Matching model—Fombrun et al. (1984) propounded this model at the Michigan Business School. The model indicates that the organization's structure and human resource systems should be managed harmoniously with its strategy. The business strategy is placed on the central stage, which showed that HR strategies should be highly calculative regarding the required human resource and in line with organizational structure to achieve the organization's goals. Also, economy, politics, and culture are considered influencing factors in this model. The starting point in the Michigan Model is that the business strategy must be achieved using available resources and organizational structure in relation to recruitment and selection, performance management, rewards, development, and performance.

Overview of Competence-Based Human Resource Management

Competence-Based Human Resource Management (CBHRM) is developed from integrating two concepts discussed above: competence and human resource management (HRM). Competence is considered to be an essential concern in HRM function to improve and evaluate employee performance. Competence represents the language of performance and can be learned in many different contexts (Rankin, 2002).

Since the beginning of the 1990s, CBHRM has been actively practiced in the USA, European Countries, and worldwide (Sienkiewicz et al., 2014). CBHRM is a blended policy, practice, and system that is reliable to utilize employees' competence as a center, which influences employee's behavior, attitudes, and performance (Gerhart et al., 2014; Suwarsi et al., 2014). CBHRM is a powerful way to reinvent traditional HRM (Rothwell, 2012). In other words, CBHRM is an application of HRM, which focuses more on the people than the jobs themselves (Audenaert et al., 2014). With CBHRM, we will put the right man in the right jobs in the right numbers (Gunawan et al., 2018) (Table 2.1).

CBHRM is the best system to increase employees' performance and to improve the organization's effectiveness. With CBHRM, we understand every human is unique with their strengths and weaknesses. Matching their strengths with the jobs and addressing their weaknesses is the crucial thing to do. Mostly middle and top managers (from outside of the HR department) and representatives of the HR managers are responsible for the development and implementation of competence-based human

Table 2.1 Differences between traditional HRM and competence-based HRM

Traditional HRM	*Competence-based HRM*
• Job analysis is the foundation or operating system of all traditional HR management • Job description is the result of a job analysis • Job description tells people what to do, which may not be fit in today's world	• Competency modeling is the operating system • With CBHRM, we could differentiate best-in-class (exemplary) and fully successful (average) performers • Matching the right people with the right skills to the right jobs or matching talent to an organization's needs

resource management (CBHRM) strategy (Sienkiewicz et al., 2014). CBHRM is the application of HRM with competence as the core.

Two Schemes of CBHRM

Centralized CBHRM—all HRM practices are in the HR department under the responsibility of HR managers, HR specialists, or middle managers (Gunawan et al., 2019). First-line managers in this scheme are not involved, especially when they have low skills in people management. This scheme is most likely to be applied at a bigger organization due to the vertical hierarchy in such organizations (Brewster et al., 2015).

Decentralized CBHRM—all organization elements, including top managers, middle managers, first-line managers, HR managers, specialists, and employees, are involved in decentralized CBHRM. In this scheme, middle managers or HR managers supervise first-line managers as the first alignment. Secondly, first-line managers implement HR practices to employees and are followed by the alignment between employees' performance with the outcomes. In this scheme, all elements are trained to be responsible for their jobs and focus on their competence. Thus, this scheme fits with the organization that prioritize improving their employees' performance, specifically for first-line managers as the direct implementer of HRM with the staff in the field (Hondeghem & Vandermeulen, 2000). HR practice's success in this scheme most likely relies on the excellent and poor performance of the first-line managers (Guest & King, 2004). Purcell et al. (2003), Armstrong (2010) said that it doesn't matter how well-conceived HR policies and practices are; without proper implementation, nothing gets accomplished.

Best Practice and Best-Fit Approach

Best practice approach—this model is based on the universalist view that there is a set of HRM practices that are universal in the sense they are best in any situation and adopting them will lead to high-organizational performance, regardless of the settings and the contexts of the organization (Armstrong, 2010). It is also called "one standard for all" or "one size fits all" (Armstrong, 2010). Pfeffer and Davis-Blake (1987) provide lists of best practice approaches in human resource management, including selective hiring, security, self-managed teams, performance-based compensation, training, sharing information, and employee adjustment. However, many experts have criticized this approach. Cappelli and Crocker-Hefter (1996) observed that each organization has a different policy and practice; therefore, the term best practice is overstated. Purcell (1999) also stated that the best practice approach may not fit with each organization's working practice, philosophy, strategy, culture, technology, and any other factors. And Becker and Gerhart (1996) said that they prefer "good practice" rather than "best practice" to describe the principles beyond the choices of practices.

Best-fit approach is a variant from precedent models of Harvard, Michigan, and York for HRM (Sparrow & Hiltrop, 1994). This approach responds to the fact that there are no universal characteristics, core practices, models, and HRM dimensions. This approach is the opposite of the best practice model. The best-fit approach means the HR strategies are in line with the contexts of an organization, which include philosophy, goals, characteristics of employees, organizational structures, cultures, technology, business strategy, and other factors (Armstrong, 2010; Boxall et al., 2007; Dyer & Holder, 1998).

CBHRM System: Structure, Process, and Outcome

Structure—Human resource (HR) activities are driven by HRM strategy and HRM policy developed by top management in an organization, and must align with the business strategy. However, all these strategies are also influenced by many elements, such as organizational factors, labor market, stakeholder interest, and workforce characteristics, which can be considered structures in the CBHRM system (Armstrong, 2010; Boxall et al., 2007; Storey, 1992). Additional elements include the labor market, task technologies, stakeholder interest, workforce characteristics, and HR competence.

Process—HR activities focusing on the use of competence analysis are the heart of the competence-based HRM model. At this point, we emphasize decentralized CBHRM with the involvement of line managers. HR managers, HR specialists, and middle managers should effectively supervise, coach, build and improve line managers' competence and performance, impacting organizational and financial outcomes. The competence and performance of HR managers are seen in their

HR activities. However, HR activities in each organization are different (Armstrong, 2006, 2010).

Outcomes—the outcomes of CBHRM fall into three categories—(1) Employee outcome. The use of a competence focus in the HRM model ensures that all employees maximally perform their jobs (Hijazeh, 2011). Therefore, it is understandable that effective CBHRM can increase employees' outcomes while poor CBHRM could lower the outcomes. The employee outcomes, according to literature, include employee competence (Fey et al., 2000; Park et al., 2003; Wright & Nishii, 2007), performance (Ali et al., 2014; Hassan, 2016; Jouda et al., 2016), retention (Aldamoe et al., 2012; Al-Khasawneh, 2013; Fey et al., 2000; Savaneviciene & Stankeviciute, 2012), motivation (Fey et al., 2000; Park et al., 2003), and job satisfaction (Ali et al., 2014; Marescaux et al., 2012; Purcell, 2003); (2) Organizational outcome. Alusa and Kariuki (2015) found that good HR practices improve employees' performance, which in turn develops positive organizational outcomes. Literature shows that CBHRM has an impact on healthcare quality (Arevshatian et al., 2014; Elarabi & Johari, 2014; Khatri et al., 2017; Shantz et al., 2016), patient safety (Arevshatian et al., 2014; Shantz et al., 2016), and patient satisfaction (Oppel et al., 2017; Ott & van Dijk, 2005; Vermeeren et al., 2014); (3) Financial outcome. Vermeeren et al. (2014) revealed that HR practices have a direct effect on financial outcomes and a significant effect on the bottom line (Savaneviciene & Stankeviciute, 2012; Vermeeren et al., 2014).

Components of CBHRM Practice

Despite the different perspectives between the *best fit* and the *best practice* approaches. Various HR practices exist today and different among organizations. The authors present multi-components of HR practices as part of the CBHRM process for reference, so the readers can compare and contrast which components fit their organizations (Table 2.2).

CONCLUSION

The concept of HRM has evolved throughout centuries according to the need, workforce characteristics, culture, environment, politics, business, and other related factors. As nurse managers or HR managers, we need to apply the HRM model wisely and strategically for the success of the

Table 2.2 Components of CBHRM practice

Authors	Components of CBHRM practice
Quansah (2013)	Recruitment and selection, compensation (pay) and rewards, training and development, employment security, performance appraisal, employee participation (voice), career planning
Edgar and Geare (2005)	Selection/promotion/placement process; rewards process; development process; and appraisal process
Guchait (2007)	Training, performance appraisal, staffing, rewards, benefits, working condition, equal employment opportunity, and information sharing
Singh and Jain (2014)	Manpower planning practices, training and development practices, performance appraisal practices, compensation and incentive practices, unionization practices, teamwork and employee participation practices
Simachew (2014)	Training and development, career development, organizational development, performance appraisal
Azzeh and Nuaimi (2015)	Training and performance development, HR planning, recruitment, rewarding and motivation, performance monitoring and evaluation
Audenaert et al. (2014)	Training and development, recruitment and selection, remuneration, performance appraisal, and other HRM processes
Armstrong (2006)	Performance management, learning and development, recruitment, selection
Smeenk et al. (2006)	Performance appraisal, decentralization, compensation, management style, participation, employment security, communication, training/development, and social interactions
Stern (2010)	Retention, recruitment, succession planning, selection, and placement
Syed et al. (2014)	Recruitment and selection, training and development, compensation and rewards, the participation of employees, and performance appraisal
Abdullah et al. (2009)	Training and development, teamwork, employee's security, HR planning, performance appraisal, compensation/incentives
Vermeeren et al. (2014)	Teamwork, autonomy, job design, performance-related pay, training and development
Brewster et al. (2015)	Recruitment and selection, pay and benefits, training and development, workforce expansion or reduction, industrial relations

(continued)

Table 2.2 (continued)

Authors	Components of CBHRM practice
Marescaux et al. (2012)	Training, development appraisal, career development, direct employee participation, mentoring
Fey et al. (2007)	Decentralization, incentive systems, complaint resolution system, job security, internal promotion, employee training, and career planning
Vlachos (2009)	Selective hiring, self-managed teams, compensation policy, information sharing, job security, and extensive training

organization. There is no golden rule in the implementation of HRM; however, the authors emphasize the use of the Competence Model in HRM to best fit with the competence needs of nurses. This emphasis encompasses all human resource practices: the recruitment and selection, training and development, rewards and benefits, performance appraisal, and career planning and development for nursing resources. Despite the multiple components in HRM, HR, and nurse managers can either add or remove components based on the organization's needs.

References

Abdullah, Z., Ahsan, N., & Alam, S. S. (2009). The effect of human resource management practices on business performance among private companies in Malaysia. *International Journal of Business and Management*, 4(6), 65–72. https://doi.org/10.5539/ijbm.v4n6p65.

Aldamoe, F. M. A., Yazam, M., & Ahmid, K. B. (2012). The mediating effect of HRM outcomes (employee retention) on the relationship between HRM practices and organizational performance. *International Journal of Human Resource Studies*, 2(1), 75.

Al-Khasawneh, A. L. (2013). The relation between human resource management (HRM) strategies and job loyalty as practiced at the public relations (PR's) units in the Government Ministries of Jordan. *Journal of Management Research*, 5(3), 146–168.

Ali, N., Kakakhel, S. J., Rahman, W., & Ahsan, A. (2014). Impact of human resource management practices on employees' outcomes (Empirical evidence from Public Sector Universities of Malakand Division, KPK, Pakistan). *Life Science Journal*, 11(4), 68–77.

Alusa, K., & Kariuki, A. (2015). Human resource management practices, employee outcome and performance of Coffee Research Foundation, Kenya. *European Journal of Business and Management, 7*(3), 72–79.

Anyangwe, X. (2017). *Strategic human resource management: A cross-cultural managerial approach*. Thesis. Centria University of Applied Sciences, Finland.

Arevshatian, L., Shantz, A., & Alfes, K. (2014). Perceptions of HRM practices, safety and quality in healthcare: The mediating role of engagement. *Academy of Management Proceedings, 2014*(1). https://doi.org/10.5465/ambpp.2014.50.

Armstrong, M. (2006). *A handbook of human resource management practice*. Kogan Page.

Armstrong, M. (2010). *Armstrong's essential human resource management practice: A guide to people management*. Kogan Page Publishers.

Audenaert, M., Vanderstraeten, A., Buyens, D., & Desmidt, S. (2014). Does alignment elicit competency-based HRM? A systematic review. *Management Revue, 25*(1), 5–26. https://doi.org/10.5771/0935-9915-2014-1-5.

Azzeh, D. Y. A., & Nuaimi, M. A. (2015). *Competency-based human resources management and organizational performance: Riyadh bank case study*. Master degree Thesis, Middle East University, Jordan.

Becker, B., & Gerhart, B. (1996). The impact of human resource management on organizational performance: Progress and prospects. *Academy of Management Journal, 39*(4), 779–801. https://doi.org/10.2307/256712.

Beer, M., Spector, B. A., Lawrence, P. R., Mills, D. Q., & Walton, R. E. (1984). *Managing human assets*. Free Press.

Boxall, P. F. (1992). Strategic human resource management: Beginnings of a new theoretical sophistication? *Human Resource Management Journal, 2*(3), 60–79. https://doi.org/10.1111/j.1748-8583.1992.tb00260.x.

Boxall, P. F., Purcell, J., & Wright, P. M. (2007). *The Oxford handbook of human resource management*. Oxford University Press.

Boyatzis, R. E. (1982). *The competent manager: A model for effective performance*. Wiley.

Brewster, C., Brookes, M., & Gollan, P. J. (2015). The institutional antecedents of the assignment of HRM responsibilities to line managers. *Human Resource Management, 54*(4), 577–597. https://doi.org/10.1002/hrm.21632.

Business Dictionary (Ed.). (2020). *Business dictionary*. WebFinance Inc.

Cappelli, P., & Crocker-Hefter, A. (1996). Distinctive human resources are firms' core competencies. *Organizational Dynamics, 24*(3), 7–22. https://doi.org/10.1016/s0090-2616(96)90002-9.

Dessler, G. (2006). *A framework for human resource management*. Pearson Education.

Dessler, G. (2011). *Human resource management*. Pearson.

Dubois, D. D., & Rothwell, W. J. (2004). *Competency-based human resource management: Discover a new system for unleashing the productive power of exemplary performers*. Nicholas Brealey.

Dyer, L., & Holder, G. W. (1998). Strategic human resource management and planning. In L. Dyer (Ed.), *Human resource management: Evolving roles and responsibilities*. Bureau of National Affairs.

Edgar, F., & Geare, A. (2005). HRM practice and employee attitudes: Different measures-different results. *Personnel Review, 34*(5), 534–549. https://doi.org/10.1108/00483480510612503.

Elarabi, H. M., & Johari, F. (2014). The impact of human resources management on healthcare quality. *Asian Journal of Management Sciences & Education, 3*(1), 13–22.

Ellis, R. (1988). *Professional competence and quality assurance in the caring professions*. Chapman and Hall.

Fey, C. F., Björkman, I., & Pavlovskaya, A. (2000). The effect of human resource management practices on firm performance in Russia. *International Journal of Human Resource Management, 11*(1), 1–18.

Fey, C. F., Morgoulis-Jakoushev, S., Park, H. J., & BjÖRkman, I. (2007). *Opening the black box of the relationship between HRM practices and firm performance: A comparison of USA, Finland, and Russia* (Stockholm School of Economics in Russia, Working Paper, 07-101).

Fombrun, C. J., Tichy, N. M., & Devanna, M. A. (1984). *Strategic human resource management*. Wiley.

Gerhart, B., Noe, R., Hollenbeck, J., & Wright, P. (2014). *Human resource management*. McGraw-Hill Education.

Guchait, P. (2007). *Human resource management practices and organizational commitment and intention to leave: The mediating role of perceived organizational support and psychological contracts*. Doctoral Dissertation, University of Missouri-Columbia, Columbia.

Guest, D., & King, Z. (2004). Power, innovation and problem-solving: The personnel managers' three steps to heaven? *Journal of Management Studies, 41*(3), 401–423. https://doi.org/10.1111/j.1467-6486.2004.00438.x.

Gunawan, J., & Aungsuroch, Y. (2017). Managerial competence of first-line nurse managers: A concept analysis. *International Journal of Nursing Practice, 23*(1), e12502. https://doi.org/10.1111/ijn.12502.

Gunawan, J., Aungsuroch, Y., & Fisher, M. L. (2018). Factors contributing to managerial competence of first-line nurse managers: A systematic review. *International Journal of Nursing Practice, 24*(1), e12611. https://doi.org/10.1111/ijn.12611.

Gunawan, J., Aungsuroch, Y., & Fisher, M. L. (2019). Competence-based human resource management in nursing: A literature review. *Nursing Forum, 54*(1), 91–101. https://doi.org/10.1111/nuf.12302.

Hassan, S. (2016). Impact of HRM practices on employee's performance. *International Journal of Academic Accounting, Finance & Management Sciences*, 6, 15–22.

Hijazeh, E. H. M. (2011). *Adopting a competency based human resource management system in Palestine cellular communication LTD-JAWWAL*. Master degree, Faculty of Graduate Studies, An-Najah National University, Palestine.

Hondeghem, A., & Vandermeulen, F. (2000). Competency management in the Flemish and Dutch civil service. *International Journal of Public Sector Management*, 13(4), 342–353.

Hroník, F. (2007). *Rozvoj a vzdělávání pracovníků* [Development and training of employees]. Grada Publishing as.

Jouda, A. A., Ahmad, U. N. U., & Dahleez, K. A. (2016). The impact of HRM practices on employees performance: The case of Islamic University of Gaza (IUG) in Palestine. *International Review of Management and Marketing*, 6(4).

Khatri, N., Gupta, V., & Varma, A. (2017). The relationship between HR capabilities and quality of patient care: The mediating role of proactive work behaviors. *Human Resource Management*, 56(4), 673–691.

KrontorÁD, F. T., & Trčka, M. (2005). *Manažerské standardy ve veřejné správě* [Management standard in public administration]. Národní.

Marescaux, E., De Winne, S., & Sels, L. (2012). HR practices and HRM outcomes: The role of basic need satisfaction. *Personnel Review*, 42(1), 4–27. https://doi.org/10.1108/00483481311285200.

McClelland, D. C. (1973). Testing for competence rather than for "intelligence." *American psychologist*, 28(1), 1.

McClelland, D. C., & Boyatzis, R. E. (1982). Leadership motive pattern and long-term success in management. *Journal of Applied Psychology*, 67(6), 737–743. https://doi.org/10.1037/0021-9010.67.6.737.

McConnell, E. A. (2001). Competence vs. competency. *Nursing Management*, 32(5), 14. https://doi.org/10.1097/00006247-200105000-00007.

Merriam-Webster. (Ed.). (2020). *Merriam-Webster*. Merriam-Webster Incorporated.

Oppel, E. M., Winter, V., & Schreyogg, J. (2017). Evaluating the link between human resource management decisions and patient satisfaction with quality of care. *Health Care Management Review*, 42(1), 53–64. https://doi.org/10.1097/hmr.0000000000000087.

Ott, M., & van Dijk, H. (2005). Effects of HRM on client satisfaction in nursing and care for the elderly. *Employee Relations*, 27(4), 413–424.

Park, H. J., Mitsuhashi, H., Fey, C. F., & Björkman, I. (2003). The effect of human resource management practices on Japanese MNC subsidiary performance: A partial mediating model. *The International Journal of Human

Resource Management, 14(8), 1391–1406. https://doi.org/10.1080/095 8519032000145819.
Pfeffer, J., & Davis-Blake, A. (1987). Understanding organizational wage structures: A resource dependence approach. *Academy of Management Journal*, 30(3), 437–455. https://doi.org/10.5465/256008.
Purcell, J. (1999). Best practice and best fit: Chimera or cul-de-sac? *Human Resource Management Journal*, 9(3), 26–41. https://doi.org/10.1111/j.1748-8583.1999.tb00201.x.
Purcell, J. (2003). *Understanding the people and performance link: Unlocking the black box*. CIPD Publishing.
Purcell, J., Kinnie, K., Hutchinson, S., Rayton, B., & Swart, J. (2003). *People and performance: How people management impacts on organizational performance*. CIPD.
Quansah, N. (2013). *The impact of HRM practices on organizational performance: The case study of some selected rural banks*. Theses of Master of Business Administration, Kwame Nkkrumah University of Science and Technology. Retrieved from http://ir.knust.edu.gh/bitstream/123456789/7747/1/NANCY%20QUANSAH.pdf.
Rankin, N. (2002). Raising performance through people: The ninth competency survey. *Competency and Emotional Intelligence*, 3, 2–21.
Richard, E. B. (1982). *The competent manager: A model for effective performance*. Wiley.
Rothwell, W. J. (2012). Competency-based human resource management. In W. J. Rothwell, J. Lindholm, K. K. Yarrish, & A. G. Zaballero (Eds.), *The Encyclopedia of human resource management* (pp. 45–47). Pfeiffer-A Wiley Imprint.
Savaneviciene, A., & Stankeviciute, Z. (2012). Human resource management and performance: From practices towards sustainable competitive advantage. In H. Cuadra-Montiel (Ed.). *Globalization-education and management agendas*. InTechOpen.
Shantz, A., Alfes, K., & Arevshatian, L. (2016). HRM in healthcare: The role of work engagement. *Personnel Review*, 45(2), 274–295. https://doi.org/10.1108/PR-09-2014-0203.
Sienkiewicz, Ł., Jawor-Joniewicz, A., Sajkiewicz, B., Trawińska-Konador, K., & Podwójcic, K. (2014). *Competency-based human resources management: The lifelong learning perspective*. Educational Research Institute.
Simachew, A. (2014). *Human resource development practices and challenges in public sector: Evidence from selected regional public bureaus in Tigray regional state*. Mekelle University.
Singh, D., & Jain, N. (2014). To study the effectiveness of HRM practices in textile industries. *Madhya Pradesh, India. Global Journal of Human Resource Management*, 2(3), 59–72.

Smeenk, S. G., Eisinga, R. N., Teelken, J., & Doorewaard, J. (2006). The effects of HRM practices and antecedents on organizational commitment among university employees. *The International Journal of Human Resource Management, 17*(12), 2035–2054.

Som, A. (2008). Innovative human resource management and corporate performance in the context of economic liberalization in India. *The International Journal of Human Resource Management, 19*(7), 1278–1297. https://doi.org/10.1080/09585190802110075.

Sparrow, P. R., & Hiltrop, J. (1994). *European human resource management in transition*. Prentice Hall.

Spencer, L. M., & Spencer, S. M. (1993). *Competence at work*. Wiley.

Spencer, L. M., & Spencer, S. M. (2008). *Competence at work models for superior performance*. Wiley.

Stern, D. J. (2010). *A study of competencies and competency-based human resource management: Exploring practices and perspectives of selected senior human resource leaders/practitioners*. Doctoral Dissertation, Penn State University, PA.

Storey, J. (1992). *New developments in the management of human resources*. Blackwell.

Suwarsi, S., Sule, E. T., Hilmiana, H., & Helmi, A. (2014). Implementation of competency based human resource and knowledge management to organizational culture and organizational performance implication. *International Journal of Human Resource Studies, 4*(3), 255.

Syed, N., Lin, X., Ajmal, S. K., & Shaukat, K. M. (2014). Relationship between human resource management practices, enterprise strategy and company outcomes: Service industry of China. *Information Technology Journal, 13*(4), 614–623.

Titus, A. A. (1994). Competence at work, by Lyle M. Spencer, Jr., and Signe M. Spencer. (1993). New York: Wiley. 372 *Human Resource Development Quarterly, 5*(4), 391–395.

United Nations. (2010). *UN competency development—A practical guide*. Retrieved from https://hr.un.org/sites/hr.un.org/files/Un_competency_development_guide.pdf.

Vermeeren, B., Steijn, B., Tummers, L., Lankhaar, M., Poerstamper, R.-J., & Van Beek, S. (2014). HRM and its effect on employee, organizational and financial outcomes in health care organizations. *Human Resources for Health, 12*(1), 35.

Vlachos, I. (2009). The effects of human resource practices on firm growth. *International Journal of Business Science and Applied Management, 4*(2), 18–34. https://doi.org/10.1201/b12878-7.

Weerasooriya, W. (2008). *Human resource planning in university libraries in Sri Lanka*. Ph.D. Dissertation, University of Pune, India.

Wright, P. M., & Nishii, L. H. (2007). *Strategic HRM and organizational behavior: Integrating multiple levels of analysis [online]*. Cornell University, School of Industrial and Labor Relations Center for Advanced Human Ressource Studies.

CHAPTER 3

Recruitment and Selection

Abstract It is no secret that the healthcare industry faced enormous nursing shortages even before the COVID-19 pandemic. Healthcare organizations, including hospitals, have been struggling to solve the problems, and the need for nurses has been so great during the pandemic. Human resource managers and nursing managers work very hard to deal with the recruitment and selection of nurses. Many nurses have come out of retirement to fill the gaps. Hiring new nurses is an expensive and time-consuming process so they need to ensure the right individuals are selected. This chapter discusses the concepts of recruitment and selection, followed by its concerns and problems for consideration, the role of competence model, and recommendations to hire the top talent nurses in the new normal era.

Keywords Recruitment · Selection · Nurse · Nurse manager · Talent · Staffing · COVID-19

INTRODUCTION

Even before the COVID-19 pandemic, the nursing shortage has become a significant issue worldwide. The World Health Organization (WHO) revealed the global nursing workforce was at 27.9 million and estimated a global shortfall of 5.9 million nurses in 2020 (International Council of Nurses, 2020). Eighty-nine percent of nursing shortages were concentrated in low-and lower-middle countries, with considerable gaps in South-East Asia, Eastern Mediterranean, and African WHO regions. Seventeen percent of nurses globally are expected to retire. In total, 10.6 million additional nurses will be needed by 2030 (International Council of Nurses, 2020). Some potential causes are related to (1) aging population, with the baby boom generation entering the age of increased need for health services, (2) aging workforce, which approximately one million registered nurses older than 50 years, meaning one-third of the workforce could be at retirement age in the next 10–15 years, (3) nurse burnout, (4) growth, (5) career and family, and (6) violence in the healthcare setting (Haddad et al., 2021).

During the pandemic, the global nursing shortage is worse. The significant concerns related to increased risks of infections, heavy workload, stress, insufficient resourcing, burnout, physical violence, and even psychosocial stigma experienced by nurses during the pandemic (Gunawan et al., 2020; International Council of Nurses, 2020) have become the drivers for nurses leaving their jobs and even profession, according to a survey conducted by ICN in December 2020 (International Council of Nurses, 2020). Besides, as of March 2021, 17,000 health workers globally have reportedly died from COVID-19 (Amnesty International, 2021). With these pandemic effects, up to 13 million nurses will be needed to fill the gap of nursing shortage (International Council of Nurses, 2020).

In the United States, according to the Employment Projections 2019–2029 by the Bureau of Labor Statistics, the demand for Registered Nurses (RN) is even higher. The RN workforce is expected to grow from 3 million in 2019 to 3.3 million in 2029, an increase of 221,900 or 7%. The Bureau also projects 175,900 openings for RNs each year through 2029, when nurse retirements and workforce exits are factored into the number of nurses needed in the United States (American Association of Colleges of Nursing, 2020).

In Sweden, 5700 nurses are resigning due to heavy workloads. In the UK, 36% of the current workforce considered leaving the profession in 2021. In South Korea, more than 10% of nurses intend to quit, while in Egypt, 95% of nurses intend to leave their present jobs, and 25% intend to leave the profession altogether. In Denmark, nine of ten nurses have considered leaving their jobs (International Council of Nurses, 2020).

Overall, based on the survey of the International Council of Nurses (2020), 74% of the National Nurses Associations reported their countries have committed to adding the number of their nurses, and 54% of countries have committed to increasing retention to address the current and future nursing shortage. However, this remains challenging. The government and all stakeholders in each country should support each other and commit to long-term strategies to increase the global stock of the nursing workforce. The recruitment and retention of nurses, along with sustained investment in training, fair pay, and attractive career structure, are crucial to meet the needs during the current pandemic and future needs of the population. Hospital managers, human resource managers, and nurse managers should be working closely to fill the demand through effective and efficient recruitments and selections of nurses.

Overview of Recruitment and Selection

The simple way to describe recruitment and selection is the process of identifying and filling a position; this sounds simple; however, the process is complex. Although the recruitment and selection process is considered one component in human resource management practice, the two are different. Recruitment is defined as the process of *attracting* individuals on a timely basis, in sufficient numbers, and with appropriate qualifications, and encouraging them to apply for jobs with an organization (Hsu, 1999; Mondy et al., 1996). Recruitment seeks to create a pool of suitable applicants. Once the pool has been assembled, then the process of selection begins. Selection is defined as the process of choosing the best-suited nurses from a group of applicants for a particular position (Hsu, 1999; Mondy et al., 1996).

Recruitment Methods

There are two methods of recruitment, namely internal and external methods. The internal methods consist of promotion-from-within, transfers, and job rotations. In contrast, external methods include graduate recruitment, employment agencies, recruitment consultants, executive search consultants, employee referrals, direct applications, and advertisements in the media.

1. Internal recruitment methods

Promotion from within—this is the policy of filling job openings above entry-level positions with current employees (Hsu, 1999; Mondy et al., 1996). This is closely related to career planning for the employees. They will be more aware of their opportunities to get promoted to a higher level than external prospects. The advantage of this model is that the organization will not spend time and money on recruitment and the internal pool of nurses already are well oriented to the organization and its systems. But the disadvantage is that the new position may require new skills, perspectives, or competence, which not all employees have. For example, if a clinical nurse is promoted to be a head nurse, they can be skillful in supervising nurses but may not be skilled in leadership and financial management.

Employee transfer—this process moves a current employee from one location to another to fill a vacant position. This usually happens among nurses within the same hospital, between hospitals in the same company or among hospitals with a mutual agreement. For example, Bangkok hospitals transfer their nurses (Thai nurses) to another Bangkok hospital in Cambodia.

Job rotations—this method is temporary and commonly performed in hospitals. The main objective of this method is to expose nurses to various clinical settings so they understand practice in related areas more comprehensively. The purpose is often to cross train the nurse to related areas so they can rotate to sister units, thus making them more flexible employees. In addition, they may better appreciate other dimensions of care needed by a patient population. The practice is especially useful in product-line practice models. The disadvantage of job rotation, in general, is that the nurses may not have deep skills in a specific area. For instance, after working for three years in the medical ward, a nurse rotates to a surgical ward, which requires different skills. Use of this method varies greatly from hospital to hospital.

2. External recruitment methods

Graduate recruitment—this method usually happens with an agreement between nursing schools and hospitals, in which the hospitals directly recruit the nurses before or after they graduate. Frequently, nursing schools may also host job fairs for their graduating seniors, where potential employers will have opportunities to interview candidates and promote their agency.

Employment agencies—there are many agencies, both from government agencies and private agencies, that recruit nurses to work overseas. It is because the demand for nurses worldwide remains high. Within a country, there may also be employment agencies and traveling nurse agencies that can provide temporary nurses to cover peak census times or specialty nurse vacancies that are hard to recruit locally.

Recruitment consultants—this is closely related to employment agencies. Even before the pandemic, the majority of the employment agencies may not always be active; therefore, they use a consultation service. The consultants' jobs are related to job analysis, preparation, personnel specification, sending an application for candidates, even interviewing and testing them. The disadvantage is that their service is not cheap, and internal applicant may feel excluded.

Executive search consultants (Head-hunters)—this is applied when a company needs to fill an upper-level management position. Such consultants are often used for key leadership positions that are targeting applicants on a national or international level. In hospitals, this consultant may not be usually used because most nurse managers or nurse executives are selected based on a career path. Additionally, it is not used for recruiting staff nurses.

Employee referrals—this is a recommendation from a current employee in the recruitment process. Hospitals often give incentives to current employees who help to recruit new nurses. This method is inexpensive and enjoys a quick response; however, it has a chance of nepotism and inbreeding.

Direct applications (Walk-ins or Write-ins)—individuals voluntarily submit their applications for employment in a hospital. This is usually used in a reputable hospital or a favorable location.

Online applications—during the pandemic, there is a big transition from walk-ins to online submissions. Hospitals mostly use web-based recruiting apps that allow people from outside the local area to apply to an area where they are interested in working.

Advertisement in the media and career fairs—this is a popular method of external recruitment using social media and career fairs.

Principles and Objectives of Selection

There are two basic principles of selection (Cherrington, 1995): (1) past behavior is the best predictor of future performance of an individual, (2) the organization needs reliable and valid data to confirm the quality of individual job performance. Currently, organizations use a social media analysis to check the applicants' behaviors to match the organization's needs.

The objectives of selection are (1) to help a hospital makes a decision about how well a nurse or a nurse manager matches with the job. Selection is a two-way decision-making process. A candidate has the right to decide to accept or reject the job offer or negotiate the terms rationally, and (2) to ensure applicants receive adequate information and are fairly treated.

Many countries have employment laws that must be adhered to during a recruitment and selection process. An example of such a law is an anti-discrimination law that prevent excluding an applicant because of race, religion, gender or other protected categories.

Selection Process

Generally, the selection process includes (1) *Evaluation of application forms and resumes*. This step is specifically to evaluate if an applicant's qualification matches the hospital's requirements. The basic needs and certifications, such as registered nurse's certification, learned skills, and attended courses are evaluated. For nurses who would like to work abroad, language skills and certificates are required; (2) *Initial screening review* to eliminate individuals who do not match with the requirements; (3) *Selection test* to measure the characteristics and qualifications of individuals. The tests vary among hospitals but are likely related to personality, competencies, and psychometric tests; (4) *Interview*. This step probes explicitly into areas that cannot be addressed by the application forms or tests and saves the organization time because the previous steps limit the number of applicants that need to be interviewed. The areas include competencies, motivation to work, ability to work under pressure or fit in with the hospital culture and philosophies. Peer interview of applicants by nurses is also helpful to promote staff engagement at the unit level and to enhance the applicant's feeling of being welcome by potential peers to a positive work environment. (5) *Reference checks*.

This step verifies the accuracy of the information provided by the applicants and uncovers if the applicant has had any work issues in the past that might be of concern; (6) *medical examinations* to ensure the applicants are physically suitable for the job and can perform the duties safely; (7) *Selection decisions and feedback.* Feedback is often given by those who interviewed the applicants, including staff nurses and unit managers; and (8) *Job offers*, may be made by the HR manager in collaboration with the nursing manager, director or vice president, depending on the level of hire (Hsu, 1999). In some institutions, manager level and above hiring is done by the direct nursing supervisor in collaboration with HR managers. When hired, orientation, mentorship, and preceptorship will be conducted during the probationary period (Raso, 2009).

Concerns and Recommendations

Based on the literature review and our lessons learned, we highlight some concerns and offer the following recommendations in recruitment and selection of nurses.

Complex application process—according to literature, the problem in recruiting nurses is the process itself (Kalisch, 2003). Passive candidates will not spend time in the application process or they may not have an updated resume. Passive candidates are not actively looking for employment or interviewing with multiple organizations (Meyer, 2019). Therefore, HR should make the application process efficient. LinkedIn and Facebook are often used to recruit candidates.

Pre-interview problems—there are several problems in recruiting nurses seen from the pre-interview stages of the process, which deter nurse applicants from interviewing. The issues include (1) no written response to the initial letter of inquiry, (2) no letter or note with letter of inquiry, (3) delayed response to initial inquiry, (4) letter sent asking the candidate to call them, (5) no response or delayed response to telephone inquiries, (6) phone answering machine and difficulty with un-returned phone calls, (7) extensive telephone tag; recruiter not available when told to call back, (8) placed on hold for long periods, (9) reluctance or refusal to set up an appointment for an interview, and (10) curt telephone manner (Kalisch, 2003). Additionally, factors related to interaction with information desk personnel, whether the applicant was expected, waiting times, testing, length of the interview, and interview environment (Kalisch, 2003), are also considered deterrents by applicants. Therefore, HR managers should consider these problems in order not to lose applicants from interviewing. Inform the applicants when they should generally expect to hear from the recruiter so it is not a guessing game. The institution may lose excellent candidates to another setting that has a more streamlined recruitment approach.

Old-fashion website—HR managers should ensure the department's website is exciting, eye-catching, and up-to-date. Please ensure that international language is used and a translation to the local language is available. Also, it should clearly explain the type of candidates for hire. Considering the new generation of nurses, they will check if the department is worth it to apply. An old-fashion website may make them lose interest.

Old telephone calls—technology has changed how to recruit top talent. HR managers should be open to candidates' preferred communication channels, not simply telephone calls. The candidates expect a response and an inquiry within a short-time frame (Meyer, 2019). Use of video calls or messengers, such as Skype, Zoom, Facebook, Line, WhatsApp, and others, can be used.

Lack of transparency—it has become a concern in recruitment and selection. Transparency is an essential component for the recruitment of top nursing talent. Every nurse applying for a position in an organization wants to be treated fairly, with ample opportunity to advance in their careers while earning a good living. Transparency means fair, objective, impartial, and without bias in recruitment and selection. The literature also validates that the recruitment and selection process should be without bias and discrimination (Ekwoaba et al., 2015). It is essential to provide up-to-date and accurate information about job expectations for the position in question.

Benefits—nurses want to work in an organization that invests in its employees; thus, HR managers should offer an attractive salary and benefits package (Williamson, 2017). According to research, 85% of applicants would happily accept a new job if it meant a better opportunity (Meyer, 2019).

Mentorship—it is undeniable that many of those who apply for a job in a hospital are newly graduated nurses with a lack of experience. Too many job descriptions assigned to new nurses during the probationary period may make them quit. Hospitals can offer a mentorship or preceptorship program to enable and empower nurses with their new roles and responsibilities and that will improve turnover (Blay & Smith, 2020).

Retention—it is not too soon to think of the retention of nurses during the recruitment process. It is no secret that new nurses resign from their jobs in a short time after they apply, with an average of one year. Considering the time-consuming process and cost of recruiting, HR managers should think carefully about keeping their nurses. Al Zamel et al. (2020) revealed several factors, such as job satisfaction, organizational commitment, quality of work-life, work environment, leadership style, bullying at work, family issues, and job security, which were identified to be associated with nurse's intention to leave. Blay and Smith (2020) identified barriers for retention and recruitment, including a deficient transition to practice program, excessive nursing workload, overtime and skill mix, nursing image and role dissatisfaction, the scope of practice, perceived discrimination, salary, residency programs, organizational culture, regional lifestyle, working close to home, and mature-age. In comparison, Yeager and Wisniewski (2017) revealed factors that influence recruitment and retention of nurses, including flexibility of work schedule, autonomy/employee empowerment, ability to innovate, specific duties and responsibilities, and identifying with the mission of the organization. Also, nurses tend to leave an organization because of issues with their managers (Baker et al., 2012), so manager development and support are vital to a stable nursing workforce.

Poor HR and Nursing Partnership—it is no secret that most hospitals have separate departments between human resources and nursing. The recruitment and selection of new nurses often disregard the role of nurse managers, especially first-line nurse managers or unit managers, although they know exactly what is needed in their units, especially what specific talents they need to complement existing staff expertise. Consequently, many nurses are recruited not based on their competence. Many HR managers often claim that the number of nurses in a hospital is enough based on the budget. In reality, staffing sufficiency may vary across nursing units and the needs may evolve based on new technologies, procedures, and changes in patient mix; all changes of which the nursing leaders will be much more aware. In many hospitals, the number of nurses is not calculated based on the complexity of patients' care needs. As COVID-19 took hold, nurses' workloads, threats to their health and burnout became issues that resulted in many nurses leaving the profession as well as many retired nurses being called for duty. An important lesson learned from these dynamics is that HR and the nursing department should be in partnership in the recruitment and selection of nurses.

They also should be using competence-based analysis based on the need and level of dependence of patients in making hiring decisions.

Roles of Competence in the Recruitment and Selection

Competence plays a critical role in determining how successful a nurse candidate will be at a hospital. Each candidate brings his/her own skills, knowledge, attitudes, traits, characteristics, and behaviors to work effectively within teams in the hospital. Competency-based recruitment begins from matching job roles (not only job levels or job positions) to individual nurse competencies. It is noted that every role has a different competency according to the setting, and hence, also needs a different interview assessment criterion.

Competence-Based Interview

A competence-based interview is often used to explore the competence of a nurse. It is more likely to be a behavioral-based interview as one of story-telling; not hypothetical, yes–no questions and answers. The examples of questions can be seen in the following:

> "Tell me about your experience in developing caring relationships with a patient. How did you do it?"
> "Give me an example of how you involve the family in patient care."
> "Tell me how you conduct discharge planning for a patient."
> "Tell me about your experience when you made a family or patient feel you care."
> "What five words would your supervisors or teachers use to describe you and why?"
> "Tell me about a time you led the team. How did you do it? What were the challenges? How did you resolve them?"

These examples are open-ended questions to allow candidates to tell their stories and describe past behaviors as nurses or explain expected competencies to be done. From this interview, we can see whether the candidate has the technical skills to do the job, stretch and grow on the job, and strengthen the team (Cook, 2013).

Competence-based recruitment is often called "strengths-based recruitment," which focuses more on the strengths of the candidates. Usually, after the interview, the interviewer is certain whether the candidate would be a good fit, and if they are not, the candidate can understand why (Hutchinson, 2016).

Some human resource managers or nurse managers use SBAR and STAR techniques for interviews. SBAR includes:

> **S**ituation: How would you describe the context? What happened?
> **B**ackground: Why did it happen?
> **A**ctivity: What did you do to resolve the issue? How did you do it?
> **R**esult: What happens next? How is the result?

STAR is another interview approach that includes:

> **S**pecific situation: Select one situation that illustrates the application of a particular skill, background, and its issues.
> **T**ask(s): Describe what to be done to solve issues;
> **A**ction: Describe what specific action that had been taken, clarify your role in the team, and what you did as an individual.
> **R**esults: What was the outcome? Be objective and specific (Cook, 2013).

In preparation for a competence-based interview, Cook (2013) emphasized that the candidate should avoid the myths, such as (1) all interviewers are skilled. Although many administrators are qualified, they may not be skilled in interviewing, (2) the interviewer has control. It is not true that the candidate is in control, (3) the first impression does not matter. Many interviewers make up their minds in the early minutes. The candidates are suggested to interview with confidence and look people in the eye, (4) preparation does not matter. Please do your homework. What do you know about the hospital? It is important that the candidate demonstrates curiosity about the organization and that they have cared enough to research the answers to expected questions.

Most Important Competencies

Frizzell (2016) identifies the three most important competencies to focus on when hiring nurses:

Decision-making & critical thinking—highly successful nurses are able to consider the whole picture of a patient's care and integrate information from multiple resources, such as vital signs, charts, changes in patient statuses, etc., to anticipate the needs of a patient.

Adaptability—each individual is unique, and nurses take care of different patients each day and in different conditions. Some patients are at a low level of dependency, while some are in critical situations. Adaptive behaviors of nurses are needed to provide care for patients in changing circumstances. The ability to continue to function effectively with calmness during times of change is significant to performance.

Compassion—the way the patients are treated and cared for is an essential component for being a great nurse. Exhibiting compassionate care to ensure a patient is satisfied, advocate for patients, know patients' needs, and speak up on the patients' behalf for the best plan of care play a critical role in the quality of care patients receive. With compassionate care, we could also see that the nurse treats a person with empathy and respect and not simply as a diagnosis. A Chief Nursing Officer said, "If you can get me a nurse with the soft skills like compassion, quality focus, critical thinking, and adaptability, I can teach them the clinical skills. I can't teach the soft skills" (Frizzell, 2016).

In this new normal, clinical, technical, and technological skills for a registered nurse candidate are important, such as infection prevention and control and telehealth. In addition, specific clinical skills are needed in each setting/unit.

RECRUITMENT AND SELECTION OF NURSES: EXAMPLES

In Thailand, before the pandemic, graduate recruitment and direct application was the most likely hiring approach for Thai hospitals. Graduate recruitment is based on the agreement between nursing colleges/universities and hospitals. In the past, nurses who graduated from government nursing colleges had to work in government hospitals. For instance, those who graduated from Siriraj Nursing School were required to work at Siriraj hospitals. Similarly, those who graduated from Navy Nursing Schools had to work at Navy hospitals. However, today, this rule is not necessarily applied and nurses can resign after two to four years of working in that setting. If they quit before the due time, they need to re-pay the cost of their education. For example, if a nurse has an opportunity to study for four years and gets a scholarship from a hospital (e.g., 30,000 Baht × 4 years = 120,000 Baht), they can resign after four years working in the hospital. If she/he leaves before four years, then she/he needs to pay 180,000 Baht, with the calculation: 30,000 Baht × (4 + 2 years). But, if a nurse studies for a Master degree for two years and pays a tuition fee by her/himself, she/he needs to work for two years only. If she/he is provided a scholarship from the hospital, she/he needs to work double-time, or four years. This regulation is only for the government hospitals, which aims to keep the balance of supply and demand of nurses considering the nursing shortage in Thailand is still great. However, this regulation is not applied in private hospitals, in which the majority of nurses work on a contract basis (one year, three years, or five years). Besides, advertisement in social media is still done, especially in private hospitals. Also, some private hospitals provide a chance for nurses to work part-time, not full-time.

During the pandemic, there is not much change in the recruitment and selection of nurses. Graduate recruitment, direct application, and advertisement are still used. However, when the hospitals need a greater number of nurses during the outbreak, some nurses are recruited as part-time nurses or voluntarily nurses. The majority of nurses recruited are the nurses who previously worked at the same hospital or were connected with the hospital. Additionally, the selection of nurses during the pandemic is most likely based on their competence in infection control. The majority of the hospitals apply competence-based recruitment and selection. A nurse who has a training certificate for infection control would be prioritized. In addition, some hospitals apply a job rotation of nurses in other wards/units to work at COVID-19 units.

In Indonesia, the recruitment and selection of nurses are typically based on the employee status: government employee (civil servants or called PNS), non-civil servants (or called non-PNS/PPPK), and contracted employees (Gunawan, 2019). For being a government employee, the recruitment process is based on the decision of the central government working closely with local government and public hospitals. The number of nurses to be recruited is according to the formation of human resources in each hospital in each region in Indonesia. Typically, the recruitment and selection of government employees are conducted once or twice a year. Each candidate should register online from the central government website and follow a written examination. The exam includes basic competency tests, personality, intelligence, and nationality tests. Those who pass the exam will be selected, and they are contracted for life.

For non-civil servants, it is pretty similar to PNS but with a different regulation. A non-civil servant is like employee outsourcing by a government institution with a minimum contract of one year and a maximum of 30 years. The institutions can directly recruit the employee based on the structured requirement and regulations, or the candidate can apply when job offers are available. The salary is managed according to government regulation and applied nationally. Interviews are still used in the selection process.

For contracted employees, it is different than civil servants and non-civil servants. The candidates usually apply directly to desired institutions, public, and public hospitals. The salary for being honorary employees is relatively low compared to the others, determined by the selected institutions, and varies among them (Gunawan, 2020). There is no standard regulation to arrange the amount of money received per month. Interviews are used in the recruitment.

The COVID-19 pandemic has a significant impact on the recruitment and selection of government employees, which was postponed in 2020, and it would be continued in 2021. However, the pandemic does not affect the recruitment of non-civil servants and honorary employees. Many nurses and other healthcare workers or volunteers were recruited to work in the COVID-19 units. All the processes are based on the required competencies.

In private hospitals, most human resource managers announce the job offers for nurses on their hospital websites. The applicants can either apply online or send their applications by email. There is no need for nurses to walk in. All public and private hospitals are currently allowed to receive COVID-19 patients as long as the requirements are filled and permission is granted from the central or local government where the hospital is located. Many job offers are available. The minimum requirements for a nurse position include an educational certificate (minimum Diploma III nursing), a registered nurse license, with or without basic life support training certificates, curriculum vitae, identifications, health certificate, etc. The hospitals are responsible for providing training for nurses if they are placed in the COVID-19 units.

Apart from the examples of HR management in Thailand and Indonesia; it is noteworthy that a significant change that we could see during the COVID-19 pandemic is that each hospital in most countries around the world provides a fast-track process for the recruitment and selection of nurses, from the normal one to four weeks process to approve contracts to only a few hours. Document selections and video conferencing or interviews are used. This indicates that the recruitment and selection process can be done immediately without any delays when the HR managers understand the importance of the nurses' roles. It is expected that the faster process not only occurs during the pandemic but will continue after, into the so-called "new normal era."

Despite the recruitment and selection of nurses nationally; unfortunately, the international migration of nurses globally is still challenging because the demand for nurses is so great. The closing of borders, the interruption of travel, and, in some countries, the restriction of outflows complicates the migration of nurses (Shaffer et al., 2020). Ethical concerns to provide more secure migration is also another challenge considering many predatory recruitment agencies exist. The Commission on Graduates of Foreign Nursing Schools (CGFNS) Alliance for Ethical International Recruitment Practices found that progress is being made to prevent predatory recruitment. Many process concerns remain, including high-contract breach fees and inadequate orientation (Stievano et al., 2021). The policy agreement among countries for the global supply of nurses should be further discussed.

Conclusion

Nurses are hard to get and hard to keep. Therefore, HR managers and nurse managers should work collaboratively. Concerns related to pre-interview issues, website, video call, transparency, benefits, mentorship, retention, and partnership between HR and nursing should be addressed to get an optimal nursing team. The use of competence-based recruitment and selection is recommended to hire the right candidates because, in reality, staff members prefer to work short than working with the wrong people (Raso, 2009). The HR management system should be fair, objective, and impartial in the recruitment and selection process. Hires should be strictly based on merit, knowledge, skills, attitudes, and education. HR managers should make the application process easy because the applicants do not have a problem walking away from a great offer because other ones are just around the corner. However, HR managers should understand the roles and responsibilities of nurses, especially during the pandemic. Both nursing and HR management cannot be separated. Besides, it is also noted that the COVID-19 pandemic shows us that the HR management process actually can be done as quickly as possible. Do the HR managers want to make it faster or not, or will it go back to the usual time and process in the new normal? We will have to wait and see.

REFERENCES

Al Zamel, L. G., Lim Abdullah, K., Chan, C. M., & Piaw, C. Y. (2020). Factors influencing nurses' intention to leave and intention to stay: An integrative review. *Home Health Care Management & Practice, 32*(4), 218–228. https://doi.org/10.1177/1084822320931363.

American Association of Colleges of Nursing. (2020). *Fact sheet: Nursing shortage.* Retrieved from https://www.aacnnursing.org/Portals/42/News/Factsheets/Nursing-Shortage-Factsheet.pdf.

Amnesty International. (2021). *COVID-19: Health worker death toll rises to at least 17000 as organizations call for rapid vaccine rollout.* Retrieved from https://www.amnesty.org/en/latest/news/2021/03/covid19-health-worker-death-toll-rises-to-at-least-17000-as-organizations-call-for-rapid-vaccine-rollout/.

Baker, S., Marshburn, D. M., Crickmore, K. D., Rose, S. B., Dutton, K., & Hudson, P. C. (2012). What do you do? Perceptions of nurse manager responsibilities. *Nursing Management, 43*(12), 24–29. https://doi.org/10.1097/01.numa.0000422890.99334.21.

Blay, N., & Smith, L. E. (2020). An integrative review of Enrolled Nurse recruitment and retention. *Collegian, 27*(1), 89–94. https://doi.org/10.1016/j.colegn.2019.06.005.

Cherrington, D. J. (1995). Job analysis and strategic recruitment. In D. J. Cherrington (Ed.), *The management and human resources.* Prentice Hall.

Cook, S. G. (2013). Behavioral interviews: Hire for the competencies needed. *Women in Higher Education, 22*(3), 23–24. https://doi.org/10.1002/whe.10437.

Ekwoaba, J. O., Ikeije, U. U., & Ufoma, N. (2015). The impact of recruitment and selection criteria on organizational performance. *Global Journal of Human Resource Management, 3*(2), 22–23.

Frizzell, J. (2016). *The 3 most important competencies to focus on when hiring nurses.* Retrieved from https://blog.psionline.com/talent/competencies-to-focus-on-when-hiring-nurses.

Gunawan, J. (2019). "This is 2019! But I still need to work double shifts and have multiple jobs to keep me alive": A phenomenon among nurses in Indonesia. *Belitung Nursing Journal, 5*(3), 108–110. https://doi.org/10.33546/bnj.810.

Gunawan, J. (2020). COVID-19: Praise is welcome, but nurses deserve a pay rise. *Belitung Nursing Journal, 6*(5), 150–151. https://doi.org/10.33546/bnj.1217.

Gunawan, J., Juthamanee, S., & Aungsuroch, Y. (2020). Current mental health issues in the era of Covid-19. *Asian Journal of Psychiatry*. https://doi.org/10.1016/j.ajp.2020.102103.

Haddad, L. M., Annamaraju, P., & Toney-Butler, T. J. (2021). *Nursing shortage*. StatPearls Publishing LLC.

Hsu, Y.-R. (1999). *Recruitment and selection and human resource management in the Taiwanese cultural context*. Ph.D. Thesis, University of Plymouth, England.

Hutchinson, D. (2016). *Strengths-based recruitment has changed our nursing quality*. Retrieved from https://www.nursingtimes.net/careers/your-nursing-career/strengths-based-recruitment-has-changed-our-nursing-quality-07-06-2016/.

International Council of Nurses. (2020). *International Council of Nurses Policy Brief*. Retrieved from https://www.icn.ch/sites/default/files/inline-files/ICN%20Policy%20Brief_Nurse%20Shortage%20and%20Retention_0.pdf.

Kalisch, B. J. (2003). Recruiting nurses: The problem is the process. *JONA: The Journal of Nursing Administration, 33*(9), 468–477. https://doi.org/10.1097/00005110-200309000-00007.

Meyer, S. (2019). Recruiting 101. *Nursing Management, 50*(12), 51–53. https://doi.org/10.1097/01.numa.0000605180.97596.20.

Mondy, R. W., Noe, R. M., & Premeaux, S. R. (1996). Selection. In R. W. Mondy, R. M. Noe, & S. R. Premeaux (Eds.), *Human resource management*. Allyn and Bacon.

Raso, R. (2009). CAREER SCOPE: Hiring right for a healthy work environment. *Nursing Management, 40*(7), 53–54. https://doi.org/10.1097/01.numa.0000357804.91881.60.

Shaffer, F. A., Rocco, G., & Stievano, A. (2020). Nurse and health professional migration during COVID-19. *Professioni Infermieristiche, 73*(3), 129–130. https://doi.org/10.7429/pi.2020.733129.

Stievano, A., Hamilton, D., & Bakhshi, M. (2021). Ethical challenges and nursing recruitment during COVID-19. *Nursing Ethics, 28*(1), 6–8. https://doi.org/10.1177/0969733021989180.

Williamson, E. (2017). *The ongoing cycle of nursing recruitment and retention*. Retrieved from https://mediakit.nurse.com/nursing-recruitment-retention/.

Yeager, V. A., & Wisniewski, J. M. (2017). Factors that influence the recruitment and retention of nurses in public health agencies. *Public Health Reports*, *132*(5), 556–562. https://doi.org/10.1177/0033354917719704.

CHAPTER 4

Training and Development

Abstract To enhance the quality of care, hospital administrators should invest more in their employees, especially nurses, as the frontline workers who provide direct care to clients. However, training and development may not be a top concern for hospital managers or human resource managers. Therefore, many nurses and nurse managers face pressing issues, such as quality improvement, regulatory compliance, budgeting, and enhancing staff competence. Additionally, the COVID-19 pandemic has changed the roles of all nurses to be skilled in critical care, respiratory distress, and infection prevention. This chapter aims to discuss the concept and steps for the training and development of nurses in hospitals. Barriers and challenges are raised for consideration, followed by recommendations to overcome these issues.

Keywords Training · Development · Quality improvement · Nurse · Hospital · COVID-19

Introduction

There is no doubt that a hospital needs to have skilled employees to manage the hospital operation and make the hospital successful. However, the effectiveness of employees is very much dependent on the quality of their training and development. Therefore, the hospital should treat its employees as their most valuable resource. They cannot manage the current changing technology, complex healthcare systems, productivity, and care quality needs with yesterday's skills. Thus, their competencies must be continually updated to perform in these new contexts.

Training and development is an essential part of human resource management. It is unarguable that nurses and nurse managers will be more productive if trained well (Katou & Budhwar, 2010). The effect of training and development on employee skills and competence have been documented in previous studies. Katou and Budhwar (2010) investigated the HRM-performance causal relationship in the Greek context using structural causal modeling with 178 participants. Their research put training and development under the resource and development domain that hypothetically influenced the HRM outcome, namely employee skills, attitudes, and behaviors. The results indicated a significant correlation between training and employee skills, attitudes, and behaviors. This supports the study results by Park et al. (2003) that examined the relationship between HRM practices and Japanese firm performance, with training as one domain of HRM practices. The results showed that employee competence was acting as a partial mediating variable on organizational performance. Another support from Fey et al. (2009) examined the relationship between HRM practices and firm performance in 241 companies. The study results showed that training is positively related to employee abilities. Hariyati and Ungsianik (2018) provided training to improve the interpersonal skills of 25 head nurses. The training was created based on Peplau's theory. Results showed a significant improvement in head nurses' skills and knowledge after they were given the training. Also, Yang et al. (2014) identified variables that influence nurse managers' competence among 68 nurse managers in a general hospital and found that training was significantly associated with nurse managers' competence, especially informatics competence. Therefore, investments in employee training are beneficial in enhancing the human capital of an organization.

COVID-19 has brought new challenges for healthcare workers, especially nurses, since December 2019, when the virus was first identified in humans. As a result, many nurses felt unprepared and had more risk of infection despite the lack of isolation facilities and personal protective equipment. Thus, each health worker, including nurses, had be trained in specific areas related to infection prevention and control from the first day of their work or during their study in a college or a university. This chapter discusses the concept of training and development and how it fits with the current situation in the COVID-19 era, followed by barriers and challenges as well as recommendations for consideration.

Overview of Training and Development

Training and development can be defined as an attempt to improve the performance of current and future employees by increasing their skills, knowledge, attitudes, and behaviors through learning (Azmi, 2020). The training and development of employees helps employees' and hospitals' growth. Training and development have different meanings and roles. Training is defined as planned efforts in a short-term activity that focuses on improving the specific knowledge, skills, attitudes, and behaviors of an employee for specific tasks. Training generally refers to on-the-job training or short-course training, while education refers to formal and long-term training. Training focuses on the immediate need for the role, and it helps the employee do the current job better (Pande, 2013). Competence-based training focuses on specific competencies, in which the training programs are broken down into individual courses or modules, and the modules focus on a single skill at a time.

Development has a broader scope, usually focusing on the development of an individual through a long-term activity to learn and develop new skills that align with the vision and mission of the hospital. Development has open-ended goals and does not focus on one single role. It focuses on the skills that make the employee a grown person and more engaged and aligned within the organization (Azmi, 2020).

Benefits of Training and Development

The benefits of training and development act like a domino effect (Azmi, 2020). It starts with the nurse managers. If the nurse managers are trained well and feel competent, that can affect the employees' performance, satisfaction, commitment, and retention; which can further impact the nursing and patient outcomes. Also, it will be more productive if all employees receive the training and development they need. The overall benefits are belonging to the hospital and behaving in ways that support the mission of the institution. Additionally, training and development will help employees be prepared for advancement (e.g., leadership roles) in the future.

Steps for Training

There are several training steps, namely assessing training needs, establishing training objectives, designing training and development programs, implementing the program, and evaluating the program aligned with the improvement of performance.

Step 1: Assessing training needs—To assess the training needs of the employees we first need to evaluate the competence or performance of each individual using validated tools. Additional data from surveys, patient feedback, performance-indicator review, and observation from supervisors are often used. Or, the managers can use the results of the performance appraisal that is conducted by the hospital. However, the results of the assessment demonstrate the strengths and weaknesses of each nurse, which will determine if the proposed training program will fit all or if it needs to be designed specifically for each individual. Next, based on the results, the supervisors and the trainers further discuss and explore the training priorities so the program plan will especially fit with the current and future system needs.

Step 2: Establishing training objectives—Before designing training programs, we need to look at the training objectives that should align with the hospital's goals. We also need to think of the bigger picture of what the hospital faces in the current and projected situations so that the training results will be beneficial for employees as well as the hospital in both the immediate and near term time lines (Azmi, 2020).

Step 3: Designing a training program—Several points in designing training: policy, contents, model instructions, duration, expenses, and location. Before creating the training program, we need to check the training policy in each hospital that encompasses the scope of the training and employee engagement. The contents of the training are related to the immediate and near-term needs of the hospital.

Step 4: Implementing the program—Next, we implement the program online or face-to-face based on the current situation. The attendance of clinical nurse managers, nurse leaders, and clinical professionals is a must that cannot be replicated by training modules or artificial intelligence, which provides case-specific solutions and approaches. There are many logistic issues related to providing education to staff who cover a 24-hour schedule, including providing staffing to care for patients while the learners are engaged in the program. The costs associated with the program will need to be calculated not only on direct class hours, but also the replacement costs of the participants hours in the program (Fisher et al., 1998).

Step 5: Evaluating the program aligned with the performance—There are two parts of evaluation: first, the assessment about the training itself, most likely related to the contents and instruction; second, the review of the effect of the training on employees, e.g., the increase of skills or competence assessed by validated tools, or evaluated from nursing or patient outcomes. This evaluation is closely related to performance appraisal. Another assessment is from the hospital related to cost factor analysis between investment and visible productivity.

The New Normal Training: Adjustment and Solutions

Nurse managers and HR managers understand that training in the classroom is no longer viable because of gathering restrictions in place due to COVID-19. Therefore, HR should develop a new training approach. There will be a change in the training paradigm, 70% virtual and 30% physical and classroom training. This new normal training mix includes eLearning, assisted virtual training, classroom training, on-the-job training, and virtual assisted on-the-job training. In this COVID-19 era, what nurses need is most likely focusing on infection prevention and control (IPC), how to use Personal Protective Equipment (PPE), respiratory distress, ventilator management, and mental health management program, as well as training for telehealth, since they will provide virtual care to clients in transitional settings.

Many of these types of programs may be available from trusted resources. For example, the World Health Organization (2020) (WHO) develops online training for COVID-19, which the topics are related to:

- The current epidemiological COVID-19 situation
- Infection prevention and control in the context of preparedness, readiness, and response
- IPC measures for healthcare facilities, including when dealing with suspect or confirmed COVID-19 cases (1-hour duration)
- Health and safety briefings for respiratory diseases including basic information about transmission, symptoms, treatment, and prevention of acute respiratory infections (ARIs)

- How to manage the risk from ARIs
- Basic hygiene measures
- When and how to wear a medical mask and a fabric mask (2-hour duration).

Additionally, the European Commission C19_SPACE (2020) provides a training program with the following topics:

- Introduction to Intensive Care Unit (ICU)
- Personal safety
- Donning and doffing of PPE
- General aspects and admission sequence of ICU patients
- Basics of respiratory support
- Basics of hemodynamic monitoring
- Sepsis and infections
- Other elements of ICU care
- Team care.

The methods of instruction during the COVID-19 include online lectures (LIVE or watching a recorded video) or e-learning, online small-group discussions, online demonstrations, online case studies, online stimulation, written assignments, quizzes/exams, and local face-to-face. Games related to the topics can be offered online during breaks. Also, providing training modules and recorded videos allow for self-directed learning. A new innovative approach in training is gamification using artificial intelligence that creates a near actual work problem scenario with a solution approach. Its modules are analyzed for winning or losing remarks as results (Azmi, 2020). Digital Adoption Platforms (DAP) also provide a 24/7 contextual and personalized learning approach with a 70-20-10 model, 70% learning by doing (inside the applications), 20% peer interaction (through virtual communications), and 10% formal education (Gupta, 2020). The duration of an online course is dependent on the materials and objectives. It can be 1–2 hours per day or 15 hours per week. It is important to check the productivity time that an employee spends in the training. Mentors or coaches can enhance learning, and can include clinical nurse managers, nurse leaders, and other professionals, depending on the learning needs of the program. Training expenses should be well-planned and matched with each hospital's budget.

Kind of Training and Development: Examples

Training and development is a part of human resource management in every hospital to improve the competence and performance of nurses. These types of training and development have been employed before the pandemic and will continue to be required in the new-normal age.

Before the pandemic, the training and development in hospitals included (1) Mandatory training from hospitals for professionals such as basic life support, infection control, risk management are on-going needs. Examples of clinical care program certifications might include acute myocardial infarction, lung cancer, low back pain, osteoarthritis of the knee, stroke, and asthma. Usually, the hospital has a clinical module for the development of registered nurses, consisting of nurse competency, lead our self, product knowledge, service quality/transcultural competency, critical thinking and clinical judgment, patient safety, nursing outcomes, delegation, and RN roles and responsibilities. The time of training varies depending on the goals; (2) Pre-service training according to each unit's needs; (3) Talent program, which is usually conducted for four months. This is a mentoring program conducted by senior nurses to junior nurses in a hospital; (4) Nurse residency program (3-year program) during the weekends. The curriculum consists of five categories, including transition topics, professional topics, clinical topics, critical care nursing practice, and leadership; (5) Induction training (results-oriented); (6) In-service training; (7) On-the-job training; (8) Training from universities or schools; (8) Competency training; (9) Online training (online class, visual stimulation, preceptor for talent group); (10) Shift-to-shift training; (11) Routine to Research (R2R) program (evidence-based practice); (12) Coaching program; (13) Apprenticeship training; (14) Job instruction training; (15) Leadership training; and (16) Foreign language training. Besides, each nurse has an opportunity to continue education for a master's or doctoral program. Whether the hospital offers monetary support for additional degrees depends on the organization's needs. It is noteworthy that every hospital needs to set up the timing and content of its training, based on the need. There is no universal time and content for each training.

During the pandemic, training for infection control (IC) is extensively demanded due to the shortage of IC certified nurses. At the first stage of the pandemic, health professionals in each hospital set up training for infection control according to the evidence-base and then updated information about COVID-19 as the knowledge of this novel virus became known. During the outbreak, all training was conducted fully online, in which IC nurses recorded video and trainees did self-training. But today, when the number of cases is low but not absent (the new normal), the training for infection control is conducted in a hybrid fashion; both online and offline. The training varies; some hospitals conduct training for one week, while other hospitals conduct the training for one month. In the critical care unit, the training is usually performed once a week in the morning by one IC nurse and one anesthetist. The training topics are related to PPE (Personal Protective Equipment), specimen collection, and all procedures to take care of patients with COVID-19, such as positioning, tubing, patient transfer, CPR, ventilator management, and laboratory. Likewise, disaster medicine principles, such as surge capacity, scarce resource allocation, triage, and the ethical dilemmas of rationing medical care, etc. need to be taught on an on-going basis.

Barriers and Challenges for Training and Development and Recommendations to Overcome

Based on our experience, there are several barriers and challenges in training and development in the following descriptions. We provide a recommendation for each obstacle and challenge.

Budget constraints—most likely, it was the first barrier in the training and development at the on-set of the pandemic because hospitals had not budgeted for their employees' training related to Covid-19. The direct training budget is related to fees for trainers, speakers' transportation and accommodations, venues for training, food and beverage, technical fees, etc. The major cost of training, however, is the employee salaries to cover their hours in class as well as the costs of replacing care hours on the units. The pandemic has forced us to adopt virtual training for nurses, and this will reduce the budget somewhat. The training providers or coordinators only need to prepare the trainers' fees and an online videoconference platform that allows many participants to join unlimited time—the platform such as Zoom, Google Meet, Google Hangout, Skype Meeting, etc. If the training requires a face-to-face meeting, inside-hospital training among nurses could be done. Internal senior nurse managers, senior nurses, or physicians can become trainers or speakers. If the budget is minimal or when a unit missed a yearly hospital budget planning because an unexpected training need arose, nurses in a unit may joint-venture to conduct their own training. However, it may be challenging because it requires high awareness of teamwork and togetherness among nurses and the leadership and competence of the first-line nurse managers (Gunawan et al., 2019). Besides, the head nurses should have a well-planned training budget for their unit ready before bringing them to the yearly budgeting meeting.

Discontinued effort—most hospitals, during the recruitment and selection process, often make their best efforts to spend resources and time to attract the nurse candidates, but once the nurses are hired, these efforts may reduce or even stop. This is the reason why nurses often leave hospitals. We know that the recruitment process is costly and time-consuming, but the continued efforts should continue to retain the nurses. To cope with this problem, both nurses and the hospital need to sign a contract agreement or a memorandum of understanding about training and opportunities, and career plans, so each nurse will be treated equally. However, a higher commitment of HR managers and nurse managers to support their nurses is needed. Clear and transparent communication is required between employers and employees.

A weak organizational culture—It is noted that an organizational culture that does not facilitate the implementation of training and development, creates an absence of a learning atmosphere that makes it difficult for employees to adjust and adapt to newer innovations and advanced technologies, as well as harder to adopt evidence-based practices, which in turns leads to poor performance. Organizational culture is defined as the shared beliefs, values, and patterns of behavior that enable a hospital to survive in a complex environment (Curry et al., 2018). Culture is socially learned and transmitted by members in an organization, and in this case, it is from the leaders, with their leadership styles (Tsai, 2011). The hospital leaders and nurse leaders provide the rules of behavior within a hospital, guide nurse staff knowing what to do and what not to do at their work, such that the behavior of both will be in line with organizational culture (Tsai, 2011). When the values, beliefs, and behaviors are unified, a positive organizational culture will emerge. Please bear in mind that the core of the value in the organization begins with its leadership.

Lack of robust training department—sometimes, although the budget is available, the HR and training departments are not creative or they don't have an adequate plan for employee training. It occurs when the HR department is not closely working with the nursing department or is under resourced. Often, it is difficult for nurse managers to convince the HR managers to provide training for nurses. Some may think that the training needs for nurses are not fruitful because the performance of nurses remains low or previous training has not made an impact on patient and nursing outcomes. Therefore, it is recommended for HR managers to include nurses in their department to know the importance of the nurses' roles, especially during the pandemic, and discuss further with them about the job responsibilities of nurses. In addition, the HR managers' competence may also need improvement. Their knowledge, skills, and attitudes should be updated regularly. The HR managers should be informed that one training is not enough to improve performance. Regular training indeed is needed, and each nurse should have the same training opportunity (Gunawan et al., 2019). Lack of training inside hospitals or poor HR management often forces the employees to get their training outside of the hospital.

Poor training attendance—although the training has been provided, most employees are unable to attend for several reasons, such as the time for training conflicts with the nurses' shifts, the training is unattractive and boring, the employees need to pay by themselves, or a certificate is not made available. Sometimes, the nurses just attend to get a certificate. Hospitals should address these barriers to the success of training and development. First, the training should be matched with the nurses' shift. Understandably, not all nurses will attend the training during their shifts, and therefore, the training should be conducted repeatedly for different nurse groups according to their available time. Second, attractive training should be done. Each nurse has a different perception of training. Some nurses want to have games in the middle of training, some may wish to have more motivational training, and some may want to have rewards, such as door prizes. Thus, assessment of training needs and training models among nurses is necessary. Third, it is preferable not to ask nurses to pay for the training themselves. Their salary may not be enough to cover their daily needs (Gunawan, 2019). Additional payment may burden them. Fourth, for those who need certificates, it is possible to provide them. The certificates will be counted for their credit points to extend their nursing license. However, the training providers should be rigorous in giving the certificate, particularly to those who only attend the whole training time. It is important because some nurses may ask his/her friend to sign on their behalf for their attendance, which is not allowed. The role of head nurses is also vital in this issue to continually remind the nurse staff to be honest.

Conclusion

The COVID-19 pandemic has brought us the reality that hospitals completely need nurses. HR managers and nurse managers should work closely to ensure the training and development for nurses fit with the need and the goals of the hospital. Hospitals strive to hire top talent so they should continually provide training and development for the nurses in order to retain them. The new normal training approach should be created to advance the necessary skills of the nurses for immediate and near-future needs. Nurses are vital front-line workers who guarantee the quality of care in each hospital; therefore, the hospital's image is dependent on them. Nurses are the essential individuals who should be focused on to meet organizational goals.

References

Azmi, W. (2020). *Employee training and development—The ultimate guide*. Retrieved from https://www.startuphrtoolkit.com/employee-training-and-development/.

Bradley, E. H. (2018). Influencing organisational culture to improve hospital performance in care of patients with acute myocardial infarction: A mixed-methods intervention study. *BMJ Quality & Safety, 27*(3), 207–217. http://dx.doi.org/10.1136/bmjqs-2017-006989.

European Commission C19_SPACE. (2020). *Provision of training on intensive care medicine skills for health professionals not regularly working on intensive care units: COVID-19 skills preparation course*. Retrieved from https://www.esicm.org/covid-19-skills-preparation-course/.

Fey, C. F., Morgulis-Yakushev, S., Park, H. J., & Björkman, I. (2009). Opening the black box of the relationship between HRM practices and firm performance: A comparison of MNE subsidiaries in the USA, Finland, and Russia. *Journal of International Business Studies, 40*(4), 690–712. https://doi.org/10.1057/jibs.2008.83.

Fisher, M. L., Hume, R., & Emerick, R. (1998). Costing nursing education programs: It's as easy as 1-2-3. *Journal for Nurses in Staff Development: JNSD: Official Journal of the National Nursing Staff Development Organization, 14*(5), 227–235. https://doi.org/10.1097/00124645-199809000-00002.

Gunawan, J. (2019). "This is 2019! But I still need to work double shifts and have multiple jobs to keep me alive": A phenomenon among nurses in Indonesia. *Belitung Nursing Journal, 5*(3), 108–110. https://doi.org/10.33546/bnj.810.

Gunawan, J., Aungsuroch, Y., & Fisher, M. L. (2019). Competence-based human resource management in nursing: A literature review. *Nursing Forum, 54*(1), 91–101. https://doi.org/10.1111/nuf.12302.

Gupta, V. (2020). *How to successfully use new training strategies for the new normal: Remote working.* Retrieved from https://trainingmag.com/how-successfully-use-new-training-strategies-new-normal-remote-working/.

Hariyati, R. T. S., & Ungsianik, T. (2018). Improving the interpersonal competences of head nurses through Peplau's theoretical active learning approach. *Enfermería Clínica, 28*, 149–153. https://doi.org/10.1016/s1130-8621(18)30056-1.

Katou, A. A., & Budhwar, P. S. (2010). Causal relationship between HRM policies and organisational performance: Evidence from the Greek manufacturing sector. *European Management Journal, 28*(1), 25–39. https://doi.org/10.1016/j.emj.2009.06.001.

Pande, S. S. (2013). *A comparative study of employee training and development practices of selected public and private hospitals in PCMC area.* Human Resource Management Department, Dr. D. Y. Patil Vidyapeeth University, India. Retrieved from http://hdl.handle.net/10603/40985.

Park, H. J., Mitsuhashi, H., Fey, C. F., & Björkman, I. (2003). The effect of human resource management practices on Japanese MNC subsidiary performance: A partial mediating model. *International Journal of Human Resource Management, 14*(8), 1391–1406. https://doi.org/10.1080/0958519032000145819.

Tsai, Y. (2011). Relationship between organizational culture, leadership behavior and job satisfaction. *BMC Health Services Research, 11*(1), 98. https://doi.org/10.1186/1472-6963-11-98.

World Health Organization. (2020). *Coronavirus disease (COVID-19) training: Online training.* Retrieved from https://www.who.int/emergencies/diseases/novel-coronavirus-2019/training/online-training.

Yang, L., Cui, D., Zhu, X., Zhao, Q., Xiao, N., & Shen, X. (2014). Perspectives from nurse managers on informatics competencies. *Scientific World Journal, 2014*, 391714. https://doi.org/10.1155/2014/391714.

CHAPTER 5

Rewards and Benefits

Abstract Nurses today are working in high-stress situations due to COVID-19. They are struggling to provide the best care and avoid the risk of infection. However, they are also working on managing their mental health. It is no secret that even before the pandemic, the nurse turnover rate was high. Unfortunately, the pandemic situation has become an additional factor influencing nurse turnover. A new setup of rewards and benefits is required to decrease nurse turnover rates and maintain a high level of competence and commitment. The human resource department is usually in charge of the rewards and benefits programs in a hospital. Many human resource managers realize that reward and benefit packages require changes, yet this needs further discussion. This chapter discusses the concept, concerns, and trends in rewards and benefits in the hospital setting in the new normal era.

Keywords Rewards · Benefits · Nurses · Hospital · Human resource

INTRODUCTION

Nurse turnover has become a significant concern during times of nurse shortages (Jones & Gates, 2007). Hospitals were struggling to keep experienced and novice nurses even before the COVID-19 pandemic. Within the first year after graduation, 18% of new nurses change jobs, and even professions, with an additional one-third leaving within two years (Lockhart, 2020). It is not too difficult to imagine why nurses leave their jobs. There are many high-stress situations and inflexible roles, which involve working long hours and a degree of personal sacrifice. The image of nurses in the community also may influence turnover. It is not surprising that nurses' job satisfaction is imperiled.

The COVID-19 pandemic has become an additional factor affecting nurse turnover; adding to nurses' high-stress work situations. The relentless nature of the severe working conditions under COVID-19, the huge number of severely ill patients requiring intensive care and the added burden of heavy protective equipment to keep nurses safe all contributed to an unprecedented work environment. As the months of nursing practice under COVID-19 have drug on into a second year, the number of nurses leaving the bedside has reached epic proportions.

There is no doubt that turnover has severe negative consequences, including losing numbers of skilled nurses and the double burden on existing staff who must work in short-staffed situations. These factors inflate the costs of nurse turnover (Efendi et al., 2019). Nurse turnover costs range between 0.75 and 2 times the salary of the individual, or between $22,000 and $64,000 per nurse turnover (Jones & Gates, 2007). The costs include recruitment, selection, advertisement, vacancy costs, orientation, training, decreased productivity, termination, low-work environment and potential patient errors, dissatisfaction, loss of organizational knowledge, and additional turnover (Jones & Gates, 2007). Therefore, hospitals must boost nurse retention using rewards and benefits strategies to decrease the turnover rate.

The impact of rewards and benefits has been documented in previous studies. Recognition, remuneration, fair pay, and wages affect intention to stay of employees in the organization (Gunawan et al., 2019; Handel & Gittleman, 2004; Parker & Wright, 2001). Literature highlights the relationship between rewards and competence. For instance, a study conducted by Katou and Budhwar (2010) in Greece found, in 178 participants, that there was a significant correlation between compensation and incentives and employee competence and performance. A similar study by Park et al. (2003) examined the relationship between HRM practices and Japanese firm performance. They found that rewards were associated with employee competence and performance. Thus, the better the reward schemes, the higher performance, competence, commitment, and retention will be.

Concept, Concerns, and Trends of Rewards and Benefits

Rewards and benefits are explained in multiple terms, such as reward management, reward system, reward scheme, and compensation and benefits. However, the content remains the same. For the sake of consistency, we use rewards and benefits in this chapter.

Rewards and benefits is a sub-discipline of human resources focused on tangible and intangible evidence of appreciation (Duberg & Mollén, 2010). Tangible rewards include a fair compensation and remuneration system, while intangible rewards include recognition, work-life, and opportunities to increase knowledge, skill, attitude, and well-being (Gunawan et al., 2020). Each hospital has its own rewards and benefits system. They may adopt motivational theories, such as Maslow's theory of needs, Herzberg's motivation-hygiene theory, expectancy theory, etc.

Several trends in compensation need further explanation:

Pay equity—This on-going hot topic remains a high-level challenge. It is not only about the salary but also about hiring and promotion. It is no secret that the wages of nurses are lower than other health professionals. The concern of gender pay equity in nursing continues; especially in the area of promotion. As nursing is still considered a female-gender profession, male nurses are often not included in development programs. Therefore, competence-based pay or performance-based pay should be applied in a gender-neutral manner.

Transparent pay—Undoubtedly, the young generation today is likely to compare how much they earn, including the size of their bonus. Therefore, the rewards and benefits should be transparently structured and based on objective performance metrics that are acceptable and understandable.

Instant reward—nurses often get performance rewards yearly, and indeed, they most likely feel bored waiting until the end of the year. The HR and nursing managers should be concerned about this issue. Rewards can be given monthly or quarterly, instead of annually. Or it can be real-time bonus pay; pay based on nursing care complexity, risk and/or technical skill needed. Imagine nurses working in the battle of COVID-19 every day, sacrificing their lives, and the rewards (incentives, bonuses) only come at the end of the year. It is lucky enough if they are still alive because their daily battles with the disease. Instant rewards can also include various forms of recognition, relaxation breaks, providing meals, and other incentives. For example, some hospitals bring in massage therapists to give quick de-stressing sessions using chair massage.

Experiential reward—the majority of employees today prefer to receive experiential compensation than material gifts or cash. A foreign trip is chosen instead of other rewards. However, this kind of reward is probably appropriate to the hospitals where its nurses no longer think of their basic needs, specifically about their fixed salary per month.

Remuneration—the majority of the hospitals are still using the remuneration system as a reward. Remuneration is a term used to refer to total cash compensation or total compensation, or even total rewards, which include intangible benefits. However, the problem is that this system is still controversial in terms of the calculation of remuneration based on competence, education, experience, and performance.

Measures—rewards and benefits will not be fair without an objective and validated tool. Instruments to accurately measure employee outcomes have become a problem in the hospitals if they provide rewards based on performance, competence, commitment, and quality of care. The compensation plan must be seen as fair and impartial and clear standards and measures make that possible.

Examples of Rewards and Benefits in Hospital Setting

Each hospital has its own method of providing rewards and benefits. We describe the rewards and benefits in terms of monetary and non-monetary rewards in the following:

1. Monetary rewards

In Thailand, for newly graduated nurses, the salary per month varies between 15,000 and 19,000 Baht. Every year the nurses earn an additional 1000 Baht. For example, in the first year, they get 1000 baht, and in the second year, they get 2000 Baht. And it keeps increasing every year. Each nurse is required to have 20 shifts per month. Additional monthly money is also obtained on a regular basis. The nurses who work on the day shift get a bonus of 300 Baht, and those who work on the night shift get 350 baht. There is no financial bonus for those who work on the morning shift or at the weekend. For nurses who work overtime (OT), they get 600–1000 Baht per shift. Overtime means nurses work more than the average number of shifts (20 shifts) per month. For nurses working in the COVID-19 unit, during the first three months of the COVID-19 pandemic, some hospitals gave 1000 Baht incentives per shift, and some hospitals gave a top-up of 300 Baht for morning shift and 650 Baht for afternoon and night shifts. Additionally, nurses with a master's degree get an incentive of 2000 Baht more per month from their fixed salary, while nurses with APN (Advanced Practice Nurse) get an incentive of 3000 Baht per month. Besides, for nurses who can speak English or another language, they can get another incentive per month, approximately 1000–2000 Baht, mostly in private hospitals. The level of salary also depends on the level of the nurses' position, according to their career path.

In Indonesia, the salary for nurses depends on the employee's status: government employee and non-government employee. For the government employee, the salary ranges between 200 and 400 USD per month, while for the non-government employee, the salary ranges between 100 and 165 USD per month until their employers offer salary increases (Gunawan, 2019). Typically, rewards given to nurses are most likely in the form of remuneration as incentive (in terms of money) for nurses. The remuneration is given based on performance, educational level, competence, length of employment, achievement, services, certification, functional position, and staff classification, which all combine into an index score. One index equals to 75.000 IDR (6 USD) (Gunawan et al., 2020).

During the COVID-19 pandemic, all healthcare workers in Indonesia who provide direct care to COVID-19 patients, including nurses, will be given incentives directly from the central government, depending on the type and place of work. As of May, 2021, the process is still ongoing to give these bonuses until all healthcare workers have been remunerated. Some healthcare workers in several hospitals still have not received the incentives; therefore, the government just announced it will directly transfer the financial bonus to each individual's bank account for a faster process. The financial bonus for a nurse or a midwife is 7.5 million IDR or 524 USD/month and for a physician is 698 USD/month (Saptoyo, 2021). This bonus is for those who continued working during the pandemic. As of May 2021, there are no non-monetary awards for healthcare workers in Indonesia.

According to a study by Williams et al. (2020) that measured 36 countries in Canada and Europe in supporting healthcare workers during the pandemic, it was found that 19 countries have provided financial bonuses beyond regular payments or salaries, including bonuses and pay rises. For example, in Armenia and Estonia, bonus payments for staff have been paid by individual hospitals. In Belarus, Lithuania, and Montenegro, healthcare workers working with COVID-19 patients have been granted a temporary salary increase during the crisis. In Canada, the federal government, provinces, and territories have agreed to share wage bonuses for essential workers (Williams et al., 2020). Generally, the monetary reward is in the form of one-time bonus payments (e.g., Greece, France, Germany, Hungary, Italy).

2. Non-monetary rewards

In Thailand, nurses who perform better will be named as "Champion," "Prominent," and "Talent Actress" from hospitals, nursing departments, and even from the Thailand Nursing Council. They will also be promoted to the next level of their career ladder, which undoubtedly leads to a higher salary. In addition, some hospitals provide non-monetary rewards in the forms of cosmetic services, massage, spa, and other convenience services as well as travel overseas for nursing conferences, short training, or short courses. Some hospitals provide discounts for treatment if nurses get sick or provide health insurance. Besides, there is government recognition for nurses who work during the COVID-19 outbreak and offer them to be government officers. As of January 2021, ten nurses have become government officers.

In other countries, based on the findings of Williams et al. (2020), 25 countries provided mental health support for healthcare workers offered by psychiatrists and psychologists. In Malta, an in-house psychologist is available to give a short and interactive session on resilience and essential self-care skills as well as mindfulness sessions. These mental health supports are organized at the national level (e.g., France, San Marino, United Kingdom), at the regional level (e.g., Denmark and Belgium), are provided by professional associations (e.g., Ireland, Turkey, Poland), or by universities (e.g., Hungary and Croatia) (Williams et al., 2020). Further, remote counseling sessions are also available to managing stress, prevent burnout, and provide other mental health supports. Apps and online services are available, such as in Finland, Romania, Norway, and UK (Williams et al., 2020).

Other rewards include free accommodation in Turkey, free access to public transport in Hungary and some parts of the UK, free hire bikes from a city-wide cycle scheme in London, and free parking near health facilities in Helsinki (Williams et al., 2020). In addition, another reward such as 50 Continuing Medical Education (CME) is given to doctors, dentists, pharmacists, and nurses working during the pandemic (Williams et al., 2020).

CONCLUSION

As we adapt to the new normal, rewards and benefits program in the hospitals require changes. The complex work of nurses in the battle of COVID-19 need to be appreciated, one of which is by providing appropriate rewards. Pay equity and transparent pay are the most concerns among nurses that need to be addressed. Competence-based pay is recommended rather than based on position and experience. A validated tool to measure competence and performance also needs to be developed to fit with the reward system. Additionally, what nurses want today for their rewards is more likely to be related to instant rewards than annual rewards and material/experiential rewards. However, if the hospitals could provide both monetary and non-monetary rewards for nurses, it would be great news for them despite burnout, fatigue, and mental health problems they face every day. HR managers and nurse managers should work closely to determine the types of rewards needed for nurses and objectively provided based on their competence. Now that nurses are being compensated during COVID-19, it may be very hard to take away these bonuses without loss of nurses in the new normal era.

REFERENCES

Duberg, C., & Mollén, M. (2010). *Reward systems within the health and geriatric care sector* (Bachelor's thesis), University of Gothernburg, Germany.

Efendi, F., Kurniati, A., Bushy, A., & Gunawan, J. (2019). Concept analysis of nurse retention. *Nursing & Health Sciences, 21*(4), 422–427. https://doi.org/10.1111/nhs.12629

Gunawan, J. (2019). "This is 2019! But I still need to work double shifts and have multiple jobs to keep me alive": A phenomenon among nurses in Indonesia. *Belitung Nursing Journal, 5*(3), 108–110. https://doi.org/10.33546/bnj.810

Gunawan, J., Aungsuroch, Y., & Fisher, M. L. (2019). Competence-based human resource management in nursing: A literature review. *Nursing Forum, 54*(1), 91–101. https://doi.org/10.1111/nuf.12302

Gunawan, J., Aungsuroch, Y., Fisher, M. L., McDaniel, A. M., & Marzilli, C. (2020). Managerial competence of first-line nurse managers in public hospitals in Indonesia. *Journal of Multidisciplinary Healthcare, 13*, 1017. https://doi.org/10.2147/jmdh.s269150

Handel, M. J., & Gittleman, M. (2004). Is there a wage payoff to innovative work practices? *Industrial Relations: A Journal of Economy and Society, 43*(1), 67–97. https://doi.org/10.2139/ssrn.199972

Jones, C., & Gates, M. (2007). The costs and benefits of nurse turnover: A business case for nurse retention. *The Online Journal of Issues in Nursing, 12*(3). https://doi.org/10.3912/OJIN.Vol12No03Man04

Katou, A. A., & Budhwar, P. S. (2010). Causal relationship between HRM policies and organisational performance: Evidence from the Greek manufacturing sector. *European Management Journal, 28*(1), 25–39. https://doi.org/10.1016/j.emj.2009.06.001

Lockhart, L. (2020). Strategies to reduce nursing turnover. *Nursing Made Incredibly Easy, 18*(2), 56. https://doi.org/10.1097/01.nme.0000653196.16629.2e

Park, H. J., Mitsuhashi, H., Fey, C. F., & Björkman, I. (2003). The effect of human resource management practices on Japanese MNC subsidiary performance: A partial mediating model. *International Journal of Human Resource Management, 14*(8), 1391–1406. https://doi.org/10.1080/0958519032000145819

Parker, O., & Wright, L. (2001). Pay and employee commitment: The missing link-The company that enhances compensation conditions and practices will likely see an improvement in employee commitment. *Ivey Business Journal, 65*(3), 70–73.

Saptoyo, R. D. A. (2021). Incentives for health workers during the COVID-19 Pandemic. *Kompas.com*. Retrieved from https://www.kompas.com/tren/read/2021/04/21/173000465/besaran-insentif-tenaga-kesehatan-selama-pandemi-covid-19?page=all

Williams, G., Scarpetti, G., Bezzina, A., Vincenti, K., Grech, K., Kowalska-Bobko, I., . . . Maier, C. (2020). How are countries supporting their health workers during COVID-19? *Eurohealth, 26*(2), 58–62.

CHAPTER 6

Performance Appraisal

Abstract There is no doubt that performance appraisal is an essential human resource management process to improve nurses' performance. However, the COVID-19 pandemic has brought a tremendous challenge in completing performance appraisals in a hospital setting. It has also been questioned whether performance appraisals are needed in the middle of the COVID-19 crisis. This chapter prompts a discussion about the concept of performance appraisal and its model in a hospital context. Some concerns are raised, and recommendations are proposed for consideration.

Keywords Performance appraisal · Nurses · Human resource management

INTRODUCTION

The COVID-19 pandemic has proved to be the biggest game-changer and a disruptor across the global economy. Nurses have become heroes in the battle of the virus, and their hard work must be appreciated (Gunawan, Aungsuroch, & Fisher, 2020). It is no secret that nurses' jobs during COVID-19 have increased due to the high number of cases and the complexities of caring for huge numbers of critically ill patients.

© The Author(s), under exclusive license to Springer Nature Singapore Pte Ltd. 2022
Y. Aungsuroch et al., *Redesigning the Nursing and Human Resource Partnership*, https://doi.org/10.1007/978-981-16-5990-4_6

Burnout, stress, and depression among nurses have become the main issues (Marzilli, 2021). Some nurses leave their jobs and even their profession. One view is that performance appraisal might not be appropriate to do during the pandemic. However, more than one year of the pandemic has passed, and nursing work has been completely changed in its wake. Nurses' work will not return to past models, but instead will further evolve in the new and atypical environment the future holds (Gunawan, Aungsuroch, & Marzilli, 2020). Therefore, the performance appraisal process also needs to be changed because it remains crucial to maintain employee performance, motivation, and engagement.

Most organizations work virtually from home in today's crisis, which brings another challenge for human resources. However, nurses are not working from home; they are demanded to standby at the hospitals to provide the best nursing care. So, the performance appraisal remains the same; but it should focus on new approaches and an evaluation of factors used to evaluate them in this new normal era. This chapter begins by discussing the concept of performance appraisal, followed by the concerns and recommendations for better performance evaluation of nurses in the hospital setting.

Overview of Performance Appraisal

Performance appraisal, a part of human resource management, is a formal, planned, systematic, and ongoing process that aims to document and evaluate the performance of each employee in technical, physical, behavioral, or physiological terms to determine their strengths and weaknesses in an organization based on specific criteria and organizational objectives assessed by some judges (typically supervisor) (Kasemsap, 2015; Murphy, 2020; Prowse & Prowse, 2009).

A performance appraisal is often called a performance review or a performance evaluation, which lies within the HR department and line managers who deal with the practice to manage and align all of the resources of an organization to achieve high performance (Muchinsky, 2012). The performance appraisal is considered one of the most critical processes in human resource management (Sudarsan, 2009).

A key reason for performance appraisal utilization is performance improvement for both employees and the organization. The other reasons (Gunawan et al., 2019) include:

- The use of the results of performance appraisal as a basis for employee promotion, career development, motivation, termination, rotation, and transfer.
- As a criterion in research, such as test validation.
- To facilitate communication, especially to minimize employees' perceptions of uncertainty.
- As a basis for determining training needs in employees since the results of the performance appraisal determine the weakness and strengths of employees.
- As a means of documentation or track record of decisions and legal requirements.
- It can aid in selecting the best-suited individuals to perform organizational tasks.
- As a basis for performance-based pay or compensation changes.

Types of Performance Appraisal

Performance appraisal varies from one country to the next, and is deeply rooted in the social norms, values, and beliefs that affect employee motivation and perception. A few common methods in doing performance appraisal are:

Rating scale method—the supervisor or evaluator uses a rating scale to measure the performance, quality, and quantity of work of employees. Some may measure competency (knowledge, skills, attitudes). The rating scales may vary; they can be 1–5 or 1–10, with different criteria (e.g., low to high performance). The average of all scores constitutes the overall score of the employee. This rating scale can also be used as a checklist method for observation (e.g., 1 None of the time, 2 Once in a while, 3 Sometimes, 4 Quite often, 5 Always). This scale can be used for self-assessment too.

360-degree feedback appraisal—this appraisal is done by a peer. The other nurses evaluate a nurse's performance. The dimensions to measure may include skills, knowledge, attitude, personality, teamwork, caring, and leadership (Gunawan et al., 2019).

Key performance indicator (KPI)—mostly, hospitals have their own standards to measure performance, and most likely, it is based on Key Performance Indicators (KPIs). Some use Nurse-Sensitive Adverse Events (e.g., fall, pneumonia, urinary tract inspection, pressure ulcer, cardiac arrest, mortality, and failure to rescue) (Gunawan, 2017). McCance et al.

(2012) identified performance indicators for nursing care, including (1) consistent delivery of nursing care compared with patient need, (2) the confidence of patients about the nurses' skills and knowledge, (3) sense of safety perceived by patients under the nurses' care, (4) involvement of patients in deciding their nursing care, (5) time spent by nurses with the patients, (6) nurses' respect for preference and choice of patients, (7) nurses' supports for patients to care themselves, and (8) understanding of nurses for what is important to the patient (McCance et al., 2012). Suppose there are no specific nurse performance indicators. In that case, hospitals usually use general healthcare performance metrics, such as length of stay, bed occupancy rate, bed turnover rate, turnover interval, and other 218 indicators (Aloh et al., 2020).

Patient satisfaction survey—This has become one performance measure of the healthcare quality system, although not everyone agrees how and exactly to measure it and what to include. Patient satisfaction usually includes the performance of healthcare delivery (including nursing care delivery), treatments sought by patients, and care behavior, performance, and competence (NEJM Catalyst, 2018). Measuring patient satisfaction can be completed using survey questionnaires, mail surveys, telephone surveys, social media surveys, or face-to-face interviews.

Nursing audit checklist—it is used to confirm compliance with proper nursing documentation and to evaluate nursing care provided to patients. A nursing audit refers to a process of determining nursing care quality and nurses' performance. The nursing audit can be done while patients are currently undergoing treatment and after the patient is discharged through medical/clinical record review) (SafetyCulture, 2021). The checklist varies among hospitals, and it is closely related to KPI standards.

Technological performance appraisal—today, the use of technology for performance evaluation has increased. One of the new technology models is gamification. It is the use of game design elements in a non-game context (Grensing-Pophal, 2018). For the hospital that needs real-time performance management, gamification is the best-suited method. It is like a fitness tracker for work. This method also fits with the COVID-19 pandemic era because (1) gamification of performance reviews lets employers track the actual performance of nurses and focuses on immediate results, as well as helps them improve engagement and motivation (Artara & Huseynlib, 2017), (2) nurses can review their performance themselves in the real-time without any delays and in a fair way as well as allow them to unlock new badges (rewards) for their hard works

(Artara & Huseynlib, 2017; Grensing-Pophal, 2018), (3) gamification based performance evaluation offers a pleasurable and transparent experience that can increase commitment and ensures that nurses do correct behaviors and can achieve their goals (Grensing-Pophal, 2018), (4) despite to manage performance review, gamification provides nurses an opportunity to relieve stress and fatigue by engaging in problem-solving activities and active learning (Smith, 2020).

EXAMPLES: PERFORMANCE APPRAISAL IN HOSPITAL SETTING

During the first stage of the COVID-19 pandemic, all nurses who worked in the COVID-19 units or related units were highly appreciated. We could see nurses wear PPE, which is so hot, and even some wear diapers and try to eat and drink less. Most of them are at risk of nosocomial infection.

In Thailand, in some hospitals, nurses are working for 14 days; after that, they will be quarantined for 14 days. After the quarantine is completed, they will be back to work and quarantine again. Some hospitals provided hotel rooms or dormitory rooms at the hospitals for quarantine for nurses and other healthcare workers. So, after their shifts, they were back to the hotel or dormitory rooms. This only occurred during severe COVID-19 situations (3–4 months), and they were not allowed to go back to their homes or apartments, which might infect others. However, after the conditions were getting better, nurses and other healthcare workers could go back to their homes or apartments.

In their working shift, during the pandemic, one patient will be taken care of by two nurses, especially in ICU. The reason is these patients need intense care. For example, it often takes up to four people to turn them from their stomachs to the supine position every two hours, and they are unstable hemodynamically, with multiple IV drips, etc. However, nurses play important roles during the pandemic. Therefore, performance reviews were often delayed during the crisis due to the extreme workloads,

Today, Thailand enjoys the new normal stage in which the number of COVID-19 cases remains low. The performance evaluation is back on track to maintain the quality of care and improve patient and nurse outcomes. Each hospital in Thailand has various models of performance appraisal to face the new normal. The majority still use a traditional way by measuring key performance indicators according to hospital accreditation standards. The key performance indicators are calculated by assessing the quality of care, nursing outcomes, patient outcomes, nurse-sensitive adverse events (fall and injury, pneumonia, urinary tract infection, pressure ulcer, cardiac arrest, mortality, and failure to rescue), and medication errors.

A range of hospital measures are used to assess nurse performance: knowledge test, competency assessment checklist, function role responsibility in department and organization, on-the-job training, annual training hours (>40 h/year), participation in professional development, quality of nurse documentation on medical records reviewed, performance from speaking test result (interview), and particular job assignment.

Other hospitals provide on-going meetings with managers for evaluation. The performance appraisal is not only conducted at the end but also throughout the year using quarterly or half-year performance reviews. This kind of evaluation is conducted to encourage targeted growth throughout the year. The evaluators of registered nurses are nurses themselves, head nurses, preceptors, peers, and even patients. While the evaluators of head nurses are middle and top nurse managers. Technological performance appraisal, such as gamification (also known are simulation scenarios), is only conducted in nursing education in Thailand at this time. We expect this system will be applied in hospitals in the near future.

In Indonesia, performance appraisal in hospitals is usually conducted in the form of nursing audits and credentials. The nursing audit is a systematic evaluation process of nursing care quality provided to patients through assessment of direct nursing care process, performance, and nursing documentation (Ministry of Health of Indonesia, 2013). While the credential process is defined as the evaluation process of nurses' competence conducted by credential committees to determine the appropriateness of granting clinical authorization/privilege (Ministry of Health of Indonesia, 2013). This type of review is often associated with specific skill privileging for highly technical clinical areas.

The nursing audit is a part of a medical audit in a hospital; only the nursing audit focuses on nurses. The process can be varying because there is no standard for nursing audit. It is done by nursing committees in a hospital collaborating with medical doctors, nursing consultants, nursing managers, or nursing professionals from nursing organizations. Mostly they use the assessment process based on the Donabedian model (structure, process, outcome) done in qualitative and quantitative ways, such as questionnaire surveys, interviews, focus-group discussions, observations, documentation, retrospective and prospective audits, and other suitable methods. Some hospitals do Plan, Do, Check, Action (PDCA) method to ensure that the comprehensive assessment is conducted to improve the quality of care. This however may be different with the methods applied in the United States and UK, which clinical audits, standard-based audits, evidence-based practice standard, nurse-level audit and feedback/ performance reports card are used (Esposito & Dal Canton, 2014; Whalen et al., 2021). Clinical audit is mostly applied in the UK National Health Service, with the cycle of the audits include: identify the problem or issue, define criteria and standard, data collection, compare performance with criteria and standard, implement change, and re-audit (improvement checking and maintenance) (Esposito & Dal Canton, 2014). Audit and feedback is commonly used in the United States to improve nurse compliance with evidence-based practices. Common audits may address central line-associated bloodstream infection (CLABSI) prevention, catheter-associated urinary tract infection (CAUTI) prevention, hospital-acquired pressure injury prevention fall prevention, patient hygiene (such as bathing, oral care), ventilator-associated pneumonia prevention, hyperglycemia and hypoglycemia (Reynolds, 2020).

Internal nursing audits are usually conducted twice a year in most hospitals in Indonesia. Additionally, an external nursing audit is performed during the hospital accreditation process by the national hospital accreditation. During the first wave of COVID-19 in Indonesia in 2020, to our knowledge, external nursing audits were not done in most hospitals. The hospitals mostly put their priorities in providing medical equipment, PPE, masks, isolation rooms, ventilators, a sufficient number of skilled nurses, and protective management, as well as focusing on what needs to be achieved in the upcoming months of the pandemic. However, during the new normal era, as of 2021, when people are able to adapt to the new situations, hospitals continue doing internal nursing audits as usual with preventive measures. The external nursing audits are not yet being conducted. The new normal era is an opportunity to evaluate previous and current methods of evaluation and a chance to reset priorities to motivate nurses and improve their satisfaction and mental health. We believe this to be critical in the new normal era due to the prolonged stress nurses have experienced that has led to serious signs of burnout, fatigue, and turnover of nurses.

Concerns and Recommendation

We highlight several concerns in performance appraisal and offer some recommendations in the new normal era.

Useless annual performance review—the annual performance review has been criticized that it is not that useful to evaluate the employees' performance at the end of the year. Nurses will tend to have high performance at the end rather than in the first or middle of the year. Therefore, many hospitals conduct performance appraisals every four or six months, and even every week or two weeks for new nurses, rather than apply only traditional annual reviews (Murphy, 2020).

Subjectivity rather than objectivity—it is no secret that the judgment based on a supervisor's subjective opinions still exists rather than objective data. Employee "likeability," personal concern, previous mistakes or successes, competition, emotion, and mood, have been questioned in performance reviews. Seniority is another factor that a supervisor (junior) may rate employees (senior) more favorably than the actual performance deserves to avoid conflict. Therefore, the judgment should not just be relied on supervisor evaluation only to prevent bias. The use of a combination of multiple evaluations from self-assessment, other supervisors, peers, or trained raters, and management assessment is recommended in combination with supervisor evaluation.

Mistrust—often, individuals mistrust their supervisor regarding judgment due to interpersonal relationships, previous mistakes, and competition. Therefore, performance appraisal can be uncomfortable and cause tensions. The supervisor should be transparent to deal with this issue. Otherwise, performance appraisal will impact the employees negatively and lead to legal matters against the hospital.

Hawthorne effect—it is no secret that many employees will modify their behavior or performance if they know they are being observed. Therefore, hidden observation and evaluation are recommended.

Invalidated measures—to avoid subjectivity, validated and up-to-date instruments should be used. Often, hospitals still use the tools developed 20 years ago to measure the performance of employees in 2021. This may not be valid because the sets of dimensions of performance and competence, and culture are different. Therefore, the instruments also need to be updated and evaluated based on the new and current standards developed according to the current situation, culture, and policy of an organization. Each country or each setting has a different instrument to measure performance.

Negative feedback—it is no doubt that not all individuals can accept negative feedback. Some may be fine with the input and try to do better in the next performance. Still, others may respond negatively by exhibiting behaviors such as absence, resignation, or other malicious behavior. Therefore, the supervisor should understand each employee and understand how each may react to a negative comment or result. Besides, performance feedback is often not useful for most recipients.

Supervisor resistance—many nurse managers do not want to evaluate their employees; thus, they ask the HR managers to do that role. This resistance behavior exists because the managers do not want to hurt the employees' feelings, and they do not want to be a part of the judgment. This is the homework of each hospital to enhance the competence of nurse managers in this performance appraisal role.

Performance appraisal versus Total Quality Management—there is a consistent debate between total quality management (TQM) and the performance appraisal methods to justify their positions in supporting employees and improving organizational performance (Soltani & Wilkinson, 2020). There is an issue that the hospitals that apply TQM will not value performance appraisal in their HR department. In TQM, individual performance is less important than team performance, and the collective outcome is the priority. TQM is a system or process-based performance appraisal. However, performance appraisal most likely focuses on individual performance. Clarity as to what areas of performance are assessed at the group level and what is to be evaluated based on individual performance is vital in order not to be unfair that an outcome that is dependent on the system is used to assess individual work (Soltani & Wilkinson, 2020). HR managers should address this issue with a careful review of the evaluation systems.

Conclusion

Performance appraisal is only as good as its instrumentation, implementation and fit within the organizational system. If it is done correctly with a well-supported system, it can genuinely help the hospital improve the practice environment. Combining traditional and technology-based performance appraisal should be useful for evaluating nurses' performance in the new normal era. The methods of assessment should also be combined. It is recommended for supervisors or evaluators to understand each employee and provide effective communication in communicating the feedback, understanding that not all employees have suitable coping mechanisms to hear such feedback. Peer review and self-assessment should be used to avoid bias in rating performance. Also, instruments to measure performance should be validated. Gamification is recommended for instant results and real-time performance. Also, issues related to subjectivity, mistrust, Hawthorne effect, and supervisor resistance should be resolved by HR and nurse managers. Most importantly, a performance appraisal should not disregard the team's role in measuring individual performance. Individual and team performance should be measured separately and carefully.

References

Aloh, H. E., Onwujekwe, O. E., Aloh, O. G., & Nweke, C. J. (2020). Is bed turnover rate a good metric for hospital scale efficiency? A measure of resource utilization rate for hospitals in Southeast Nigeria. *Cost Effectiveness and Resource Allocation, 18*(1), 21. https://doi.org/10.1186/s12962-020-00216-w10.1186/s12962-020-00216-w

Artara, A., & Huseynlib, B. (2017). *Gamification based performance evaluation system: A new model suggestion.* Paper presented at the 7th International Conference on Leadership, Technology, Innovation and Business Management, Marmaris, Turkey.

Esposito, P., & Dal Canton, A. (2014). Clinical audit, a valuable tool to improve quality of care: General methodology and applications in nephrology. *World Journal of Nephrology, 3*(4), 249–255. https://doi.org/10.5527/wjn.v3.i4.249

Grensing-Pophal, L. (2018). *Better workplace performance with gamification.* Retrieved from https://hrdailyadvisor.blr.com/2018/02/14/better-workplace-performance-gamification/

Gunawan, J. (2017). *Nursing indicator.* Retrieved from https://www.academia.edu/10131568/Nursing_indicator

Gunawan, J., Aungsuroch, Y., & Fisher, M. L. (2019). Competence-based human resource management in nursing: A literature review. *Nursing Forum, 54*(1), 91–101. https://doi.org/10.1111/nuf.12302

Gunawan, J., Aungsuroch, Y., & Fisher, M. L. (2020). One year of the COVID-19 pandemic: Nursing research priorities for the new normal era. *Belitung Nursing Journal, 6*(6), 187–189. https://doi.org/10.33546/bnj.1255

Gunawan, J., Aungsuroch, Y., & Marzilli, C. (2020). 'New normal' in Covid-19 era: A nursing perspective from Thailand. *Journal of the American Medical*

Directors Association, 21(10), 1514. https://doi.org/10.1016/j.jamda.2020. 07.021

Kasemsap, K. (2015). Developing a framework of human resource management, organizational learning, knowledge management capability, and organizational performance. In P. O. d. Pablos (Ed.), *Knowledge management for competitive advantage during economic crisis* (pp. 164–193). IGI Global.

Marzilli, C. (2021). A year later: Life after the Year of the Nurse. *Belitung Nursing Journal, 7*(2), 59–61. https://doi.org/10.33546/bnj.1509

McCance, T., Telford, L., Wilson, J., MacLeod, O., & Dowd, A. (2012). Identifying key performance indicators for nursing and midwifery care using a consensus approach. *Journal of Clinical Nursing, 21*(7-8), 1145–1154. https://doi.org/10.1111/j.1365-2702.2011.03820.x

Ministry of Health of Indonesia. (2013). *Hospital nursing committee*. Retrieved from http://bprs.kemkes.go.id/v1/uploads/pdffiles/peraturan/27%20PMK%20No.%2049%20ttg%20Komite%20Keperawatan%20RS.pdf

Muchinsky, P. M. (2012). *Psychology applied to work* (10th ed.). Hypergraphic Press.

Murphy, K. R. (2020). Performance evaluation will not die, but it should. *Human Resource Management Journal, 30*(1), 13–31. https://doi.org/10.1111/1748-8583.12259

NEJM Catalyst. (2018). *Patient satisfaction surveys*. Retrieved from https://catalyst.nejm.org/doi/full/10.1056/CAT.18.0288

Prowse, P., & Prowse, J. (2009). The dilemma of performance appraisal. *Measuring Business Excellence, 13*(4), 69–77. https://doi.org/10.1108/13683040911006800

Reynolds, S. (2020). Using audit and feedback to improve compliance with evidence-based practices. Retrieved from https://www.myamericannurse.com/using-audit-and-feedback-to-improve-compliance-with-evidence-based-practices/

SafetyCulture. (2021). *Nursing audit checklists*. Retrieved from https://safetyculture.com/checklists/nursing-audit/#:~

Smith, A. (2020). *Reduce stress among nurses through gamification*. (Master's in Medical Engineering), KTH Royal Institute of Technology, School of Engineering Sciences in Chemistry, Biotechnology and Health, Sweden.

Soltani, E., & Wilkinson, A. (2020). TQM and performance appraisal: Complementary or incompatible? *European Management Review, 17*(1), 57–82. https://doi.org/10.1111/emre.12317

Sudarsan, A. (2009). Performance appraisal systems: A survey of organizational views. *The IUP Journal of Organizational Behaviour, 3*(1), 54–69.

Whalen, M., Maliszewski, B., Gardner, H., & Smyth, S. (2021). Audit and Feedback: An evidence-based practice literature review of nursing report cards. *Worldviews on Evidence-Based Nursing, 18*(3), 170–179. https://doi.org/10.1111/wvn.12492

CHAPTER 7

Career Planning and Development

Abstract The World Health Organization designated 2020 as the year of nurses, making that year the first for such international recognition of the crucial role of nurses in every country. Nurses have shown themselves to be the real heroes in the battle of the COVID-19 pandemic. Are nurses only needed during a pandemic? No. Nurses toil relentlessly over their entire careers. Many nurses do not actively pay attention to managing their careers. How can their workplaces provide career advancement opportunities, mentor career advancement in their staff, and work harder at retaining these knowledge workers? This chapter discusses career planning and development for nurses; its steps, concerns and recommendations are highlighted. Examples of career planning and development of nurses in hospital settings are also offered.

Keywords Career planning · Development · Nurses · COVID-19

Introduction

"What am I going to be in five or ten years, and how do I get there?" This is a question that new nurses often ask. It is no secret that a career plan for nurses is often unclear because the career ladder system in hospitals does not support their growth over an entire career. Many nurses work for

© The Author(s), under exclusive license to Springer Nature
Singapore Pte Ltd. 2022
Y. Aungsuroch et al., *Redesigning the Nursing and Human Resource Partnership*, https://doi.org/10.1007/978-981-16-5990-4_7

more than 20 years, but their positions and job levels remain the same. Therefore, many nurses leave their current workplaces, quit their jobs, and even leave their home countries to get a better chance.

The literature revealed that limited career and educational opportunities, low-wage compensation, poor working environment, unstable political environments, and lack of health safety are the push factors of nurse migration (Efendi et al., 2018). In contrast, they are also influenced by pull factors to move, including a professional work environment, career advancement, recognition, stable socio-political environment, attractive salaries, and quality of life improvement (Efendi et al., 2018; Li et al., 2014). However, it is a combination of both the push and pull factors that incite nurse migration.

The Philippines is still considered the source country that sends its nurses to the USA, UK, Canada, and other countries (Efendi et al., 2018; Li et al., 2014). Other source countries include the Caribbean, South Africa, Ghana, India, Korea, China, etc. (Li et al., 2014). Undoubtedly, they are making a global impact on to healthcare system even before the COVID-19 pandemic.

However, during the pandemic, the global nursing shortage becomes worse. Despite aging factors, career, and violence, many nurses intend to leave their jobs due to fatigue, increased risks of infections, high-stress work situations, poor remuneration, etc. (Gunawan, Juthamanee, et al., 2020; International Council of Nurses, 2020). The World Health Organization (WHO) revealed the global nursing workforce was at 27.9 million and estimated a global shortfall of 5.9 million nurses in 2020 (International Council of Nurses, 2020). In total, 10.6 million additional nurses will be needed by 2030 (International Council of Nurses, 2020).

With the greater need for nurses around the world, it is indicated that the competition to retain nurses is not only from hospital to hospital but also from one country to another. Indeed, each country or hospital does not want to lose its skilled nurses, which will affect the quality of nursing services. Therefore, nurse managers and human resource managers should have better planning and development for their nurses. Brain drain and brain gain issues should be addressed nationally and internationally.

In this chapter, we discuss the concept of career planning and development, followed by concerns and recommendations for consideration. It is in the hospital's best interest to retain talented nurses by fostering their growth within the hospital, rather than having to leave to pursue a better opportunity.

Overview of Career Planning and Development

A career is an individual's perceived sequence of behavior and attitude associated with job-related activities and experiences throughout one's life (Gunawan et al., 2018). A career path is a sequential pattern of jobs within a career, while career planning is the process of selecting one career goal or path and identify the plans to achieve the goals (Gunawan et al., 2019). Career development is the improvement an individual achieves to accomplish the career plan. So, career planning and development is defined as the process of selecting and designing a career path, goals, and objectives, as well as implementing the plans. A human resource definition of career planning and development is the process of human resource managers assisting a nurse to give a roadmap of their career. The purpose is to have a better match between personal needs, abilities, and goals and current and future opportunities available in the hospital, and to help the nurse achieve the stated goals (Gunawan, Aungsuroch, et al., 2020). Career planning and development is flexible according to human needs, organizational size and complexity, and values and aspirations. Also, this career planning and development is closely related to training and development.

Career planning and development is a part of human resource management in the hospital. Such services allow nurses to evaluate the needed competencies for specific positions and to evaluate their own competencies and potential for those positions. Additionally, such reviews allow nurses to predict appropriate positions for their career advancement (Draganidis & Mentzas, 2006). With career planning and development, better career opportunities are provided, especially for nurses who perform well (Azmi, 2010).

Career planning and development has become an important factor that influences the performance of nurse competence and performance. Career planning and development is a part of the resource and development domain that influenced the HRM outcomes, namely employee skills, attitudes, and behaviors (Gunawan et al., 2019; Katou & Budhwar, 2010). Fera (2018) reported that career planning and development significantly correlated with competence and performance in 120 nurses, reflecting their knowledge, skills, and attitudes in a hospital in Indonesia. Therefore, human resource managers should pay attention to nurses' careers and development.

The importance of career planning and development is (1) to attract and retain competent nurses, and (2) to achieve better productivity, which helps a nurse to do things she/he is good at. If a nurse is better at intensive care, do not place him/her in a surgical ward. This sometimes happens during job rotation, (3) reduce employee dissatisfaction and turnover. An unclear career path is one factor in nurse turnover, (4) improve nurses' commitment and motivation, and (5) meet the future needs of the hospitals (Gunawan et al., 2019).

To be successful in career and development, the employee and manager should work closely and understand their own roles. The employees should identify and be aware of their knowledge, skills, abilities, interests, and values. They should select the career options for their career plan based on their career goals while building skills needed for the next level they want to attain (Gunawan et al., 2019). Nurses have many choices. Traditional choices such as being a nurse manager, a nurse researcher, and a nurse educator often are the ones that come to mind. However, with advanced education, they may choose an advanced practice role or a specialty area based on their desired patient population, such as pediatrics. Besides, they also can go overseas for better opportunities.

Steps for Career Planning and Development

There are four steps for career planning and development as follow:

Step 1: Identifying Individual Needs and Aspirations

Most nurses do not have a clear idea about their needs, career aspirations, and goals within a hospital. When applying to be nurses, they may think that they will forever be in the same position without knowing what they want to be in the next five or ten years. Therefore, human resource and nurse managers should help an employee explore their needs in alignment with their competence, and what they want to be in the near future.

Step 2: Analyze the Career Opportunities

Once the needs and competence of a nurse are known, the hospital has to provide career opportunities for each position based on the level of competence. Short-term and long-term goals should be provided. Many hospitals have limited choices for their nurses, so many nurses resign from their jobs. The hospital needs to provide various positions and different levels of clinical nurses aligned with competence, education, and experience, as well as the next level such as nurse managers, specialists, consultants, or researchers in the hospital. Competence-based career development should be applied to avoid imbalance between nurses who have more experience but lack professional degrees and those with low experience but have a high-professional degree. Also, if the goal of a nurse is to practice at the bedside only, then do not force them to be a nurse manager. Advance practice nurse (APN) positions are often recommended in this situation. Some hospitals offer a career ladder for nurses that ranges from novice to expert levels with designations, such as RN-1, RN-2, RN-3, and RN-4. RN-4 is considered the top level for RNs at the bedside and include a salary increase (Pullen, 2017).

Step 3: Align Needs and Opportunities
Next, matching the needs of nurses and opportunities in hospitals is vital. This alignment is changeable over time in line with employees' needs and hospital requirements. The hospital should manage a talent list for the nurses in the career development path and encourage nurses to look at opportunities for which they are a match.

Step 4: Formulate and Implement Career Planning Strategies
This step is quite challenging because it should be in line with regular performance appraisals. The performance appraisal results will determine if a nurse needs special assignments, job rotation, coaching or empowering, preceptorship, and training for their future positions. This step should be supported by the individual career development efforts too. This should be realistic according to the agreement between each nurse and hospital for short-term or long-term plans. In some hospitals, short courses in management are offered and management positions are available for applications by nurses who have completed these prerequisite courses.

Examples of Career Planning and Development of Nurses in Hospital Setting

Thailand
There are various models of career paths in hospitals in Thailand. We discuss three models of career paths that are usually applied in both public and private hospitals.

First, there are 11 levels of nurses as the following:

- Level 1 and 2—usually for technical nurses. To be a technical nurse requires two years of education. There are some colleges open for technical nurse programs, and they are invited to upgrade their education.
- Level 3—Registered Nurse (RN) who works for three years (But in public hospitals, RN is considered level 3 once they graduated)
- Level 4—RN who works for four years
- Level 5—RN who works for five years
- Level 6—RN who works for six years
- Level 7—RN who works for eight years
- Level 8—only for some head nurses or head of nursing departments in hospitals and nursing instructors in education
- Level 9—for vice hospital director or dean of nursing college
- Level 10 and 11—for Ministry of Health

Second, the 11 levels are categorized into five levels:

- Practitioner level nurse—for RN with level 3, 4, and 5
- Professional level nurse—for RN with level 6 and 7
- Senior professional level nurse—For RN with level 8
- Expert level—for RN with level 9
- Advisory level—for RN with level 10 and 11

Third, in some hospitals, if a nurse gets to level 4, she/he can choose to be in many positions, including:

- Clinical Nurse Specialist 5–10. After level 10, a nurse can be a nurse director.
- Clinical Nurse Researcher
- Clinical Nurse Educator, and
- Clinical Nurse Manager

Or, in some hospitals, a nurse could choose to be:

- Deputy/Assist Head of Department/Manager (MN-5)

- Head of Department/Manager (MN 6)
- Assistant Manager (Division) (MN-7)
- Manager (Division) (MN-8)
- Assistant Nursing Director (MN-9)
- Deputy Nursing Director (MN-10). After this level, a nurse could step forward to be a nurse director.

To get another level, each nurse must meet Key Performance Indicators (KPIs) with 50 credit hours of Continuing Nursing Education Units per year, pass a competency test, and meet working experience. These credit hours are also needed to continue the practical nurse license. However, to be head nurses, head of a department, vice director, or other higher positions, a succession planning committee should be created. It will be further discussed in the next chapter.

Indonesia
There are various models of career ladder systems in hospital settings in Indonesia. There is no gold standard for managing career ladder paths. However, the Ministry of Health of the Republic of Indonesia established regulation No. 40 in 2017, on the development of a clinical nurse career path, which is expected to be followed by all hospitals in Indonesia (Ministry of Health of Indonesia, 2017). There are four models of nurses' career paths, namely clinical nurse, nurse manager, nurse educator, and nurse researcher. A clinical nurse (or called *Perawat Klinik—PK*) refers to a registered nurse who provides direct nursing care to patients as individuals, families, groups, and communities. A nurse manager (or called *Perawat Manajer—PM*) refers to a registered nurse who manages nursing services at healthcare facilities as first-line nurse managers, middle managers, and top managers. A nurse educator (or called *Perawat Pendidik—PP*) refers to a registered nurse who provides education to students in educational institutions. A nurse researcher (or called *Perawat Riset—PR*) refers to a registered nurse who works in the nursing/health research fields. Each type of nurse has a different level (level 1–5). To be Nurse Manager I, a nurse should be a Clinical Nurse II. To be Nurse Educator I, Clinical Nurse III is required, and to be Nurse Researcher I, Clinical Nurse IV is required.

Improvement of professional career paths through Continuous Professional Development (CPD) based on education can be done in two ways, namely formal education and competency-based continuing education (certification):

1. Formal Education

Clinical Nurse 1 (PK 1)—Clinical nurse 1 (Novice) has a D-III nursing educational background with a work experience of ≥ one year and has a clinical period level I for three to six years or a nurse with a work experience of ≥ one year and has a clinical period of level I for two to four years. Clinical nurse 1 must have a preclinical certificate.

Clinical Nurse 2 (PK 2)—Clinical nurses 2 (Advanced Beginner) have a D-III nursing educational background with work experience ≥ four years and undergo a level II clinical period for six to nine years or Ners with work experience ≥ three years and undergo a level II clinical period for four to seven years. Clinical nurse 2 must have a PK 1 certificate.

Clinical Nurse 3 (PK 3)—Clinical nurse 3 (Competent) has a D-III nursing educational background with work experience ≥ ten years and has a clinical level III for nine to 12 years or Ners with work experience ≥ seven years and has a clinical level III period for six to nine years or Ners Specialist I with zero years of work experience and undergoing clinical level III for two to four years. Clinical nurse III with D-III nursing and Ners must have a PK II certificate.

Clinical Nurse 4 (PK 4)—Clinical nurse 4 (Proficient) has a Ners educational background with work experience ≥ 13 years and undergoing level IV clinical period for nine to 12 years or Specialist Nurse I with work experience ≥ two years and undergoing clinical level 4 for six to nine years. Clinical 4 nurses must have a PK III certificate.

Clinical Nurse 5 (PK 5)—Clinical nurse 5 (Expert) has an educational background as Specialist I with work experience ≥ of four years and has a PK IV certificate or Specialist Nurse II (Consultant) with zero-year work experience. Clinical nurse 5 underwent clinical level 5 until retirement age.

2. Competency-Based Continuing Education (Certification)

Clinical Nurse 1 (PK 1)—Clinical nurse 1 (Novice) has a D-III nursing educational background with a work experience of ≥ one year and has a clinical period level I for three to six years or a nurse with a work experience of ≥ one year and has a clinical period of level I for two to four years. Clinical nurse 1 must have a preclinical certificate.

Clinical Nurse 2 (PK 2)—Clinical nurses 2 (Advanced Beginner) have a D-III nursing educational background with work experience ≥ four years and undergo a level II clinical period for six to nine years or Ners with work experience ≥ three years and undergo a level II clinical period for four to seven years. Clinical nurse 2 must have a PK 1 certificate.

Clinical Nurse 3 (PK 3)—Clinical nurses 3 (Competent) have a D-III Nursing background with work experience ≥ ten years and undergo a level III clinical period for 9–12 years or Ners with work experience ≥ seven years and undergo a level III clinical period for 6–9 years. Clinical nurse 3 must have a PK 2 certificate and technical certification.

Clinical Nurse 4 (PK 4)—Clinical nurse 4 (Proficient) has a D-III Nursing background with work experience ≥ 19 years and undergoing level IV clinical period until entering retirement or Ners with work experience ≥ 13 years and undergoing clinical level IV for 9–12 years. Clinical nurses 4 must have a PK 3 certificate as well as a technical certification 2.

Clinical Nurse 5 (PK 5)—Clinical nurse 5 (Expert) has a Ners background with work experience ≥ of 22 years and has undergone a level V clinical period until entering retirement age. Clinical nurse 5 must have a PK 4 certificate as well as a technical certification 2.

CONCERNS AND RECOMMENDATION

There are four concerns and recommendations raised in the career planning and development as follow:

Nursing Is a Needed Profession

Without any doubt, being a nurse is one of the top professions needed today. COVID-19 pandemic has changed the trend of nursing to be the top priority among other professions. Healthcare industries and companies should be working very hard to prepare skilled nurses for today and the future. This may be considered one positivity of the pandemic for nursing.

Unclear Career Path

It is no secret that many hospitals do not have clear career paths for their nurses. There are two things to point out: (1) Some hospitals may apply the recognition and status of nurses from RN-1 to RN-4; however, there is still a debate in the criteria for determining the level, mainly related to competence, experience, and educational level; (2) It is no clear path after a nurse reach RN-4. The next step is questionable whether they will go further for the next level as a nurse manager. Many hospitals provide limited options. Those who are not interested in stepping into an administrative role will remain in the same position as RN-4. Therefore, it is suggested that the hospital, specifically human resources and nurse managers, provide a clear career path or career ladder program for their nurses.

Seniority

Today's hospital comprises mixed nurse staff, in which young and older nurses work together in delivering nursing care. It is somehow challenging for nurse managers to deal with staffing and career planning and development. Many hospitals put the senior first, junior second, which provides the gap between them. This seniority has become a push factor for junior nurses to leave the job. Human resource managers should manage this issue properly.

Bureaucracy

It is no secret that bureaucracy and political negotiation may exist in the hospitals, particularly in the transition of clinical nurses to administration. The career planning that has been appropriately designed sometimes is not as effective as political power and networking. The integrity of nurse managers and human resource managers is challenged to stay on the track to advance nurses' careers according to their competence and merit.

Conclusion

As one of the world's top professions today, nurses are needed everywhere, particularly in response to the COVID-19 pandemic and now facing the new normal era. Career planning and development is one of the strategies to attract nurses, and it must be clear and transparent. Nurse managers and HR managers should address the unclear career path, seniority, and bureaucracy. Career opportunities should be aligned with the needs of nurses today.

REFERENCES

Azmi, I. A. G. (2010). Competency-based human resource practices in Malaysian public sector organizations. *African Journal of Business Management, 4*(2), 235.

Draganidis, F., & Mentzas, G. (2006). Competency based management: A review of systems and approaches. *Information Management & Computer Security, 14*(1), 51–64. https://doi.org/10.1108/09685220610648373

Efendi, F., Nursalam, N., Kurniati, A., & Gunawan, J. (2018). Nursing qualification and workforce for the association of Southeast Asian Nations economic community. *Nursing Forum, 53*(2), 197–203. https://doi.org/10.1111/nuf.12243

Fera, S. (2018). *Relationship of nurse career ladder application with nurses performance in inpatient ward of RSUD Palembang Bari.* (Master Thesis), Andalas University, Semarang.

Gunawan, J., Aungsuroch, Y., & Fisher, M. L. (2019). Competence-based human resource management in nursing: A literature review. *Nursing Forum, 54*(1), 91–101. https://doi.org/10.1111/nuf.12302

Gunawan, J., Aungsuroch, Y., Fisher, M. L., McDaniel, A. M., & Marzilli, C. (2020). Managerial competence of first-line nurse managers in public hospitals in Indonesia. *Journal of Multidisciplinary Healthcare, 13*, 1017. https://doi.org/10.2147/JMDH.S269150

Gunawan, J., Aungsuroch, Y., Sukarna, A., & Wahab, N. (2018). Nursing students plan after graduation: A qualitative study. *Journal of Education and Health Promotion, 7.* https://doi.org/10.4103/jehp.jehp_18_17

Gunawan, J., Juthamanee, S., & Aungsuroch, Y. (2020). Current mental health issues in the era of Covid-19. *Asian Journal of Psychiatry.* https://doi.org/10.1016/j.ajp.2020.102103

International Council of Nurses. (2020). *International Council of Nurses policy brief.* Retrieved from https://www.icn.ch/sites/default/files/inline-files/ICN%20Policy%20Brief_Nurse%20Shortage%20and%20Retention_0.pdf

Katou, A. A., & Budhwar, P. S. (2010). Causal relationship between HRM policies and organisational performance: Evidence from the Greek manufacturing sector. *European Management Journal, 28*(1), 25–39. https://doi.org/10.1016/j.emj.2009.06.001

Li, H., Nie, W., & Li, J. (2014). The benefits and caveats of international nurse migration. *International Journal of Nursing Sciences, 1*(3), 314–317. https://doi.org/10.1016/j.ijnss.2014.07.006

Ministry of Health of Indonesia. (2017). *Regulation of Ministry of Health of the Republic of Indonesia No. 40 year 2017 regarding development of professional career paths of clinical nurses.* Retrieved from http://hukor.kemkes.go.id/uploads/produk_hukum/PMK_No._40_ttg_Pengembangan_Jenjang_Karir_Profesional_Perawat_Klinis_.pdf

Pullen, R. L., Jr. (2017). Climb high! Career Ladders. *Nursing Made Incredibly Easy*, *15*(3), 25–29. https://doi.org/10.1097/01.nme.0000514213.30887.78

CHAPTER 8

Succession Planning

Abstract In light of the nursing shortage, nursing leaders need to take strategic action to prepare nurses to assume critical leadership roles in the near future. Succession planning programs are a key strategy for addressing the impending shortage of nurse leaders. However, the COVID-19 pandemic has changed the succession plans in recruiting and hiring nursing managers. Such planning involves identifying and preparing high-potential individuals to assume leadership roles. This chapter outlines initial steps in succession planning during the COVID-19 crisis. The succession planning of nurse managers in a hospital context is also described.

Keywords Succession planning · Nurse managers · Leadership · Role-transition

INTRODUCTION

Healthcare succession planning practices are lacking. Nurse managers are historically selected within an organization based on clinical skills. But they often lack formal leadership preparation. This is not because they are uninterested or unwilling, but because they have lacked the opportunities to develop themselves for leadership positions. Many nurses have been working for more than 20 years, but their positions remain at the same level. Some organizations do not even have a succession planning process to replace senior nursing leadership (Lotich, 2017). Therefore, succession planning should be developed to ensure continuing leadership needs.

Succession planning is a process for identifying and developing new leaders who can replace the old leaders when they leave, retire, or die. Replacement planning is defined in different ways. In dictatorships, it aims for continuity of leadership; in monarchies, it is settled by order of succession; and in business, it entails developing internal people with the potential to fill leadership positions (Menaldo, 2016). In terms of hospital administration, succession planning is for transforming quality staff into leaders and maintaining a pipeline of future nurse leaders (Titzer et al., 2014).

Succession planning aims to delineate the desired leadership competencies and identify future high-potential leaders. Effective succession planning should be integral to the organization's culture, and the process should cultivate "predictability" rather than "chaos" or last-minute scrambling to find potential leadership candidates. Succession planning considers moving through different leadership levels, e.g., local chapters to provincial/territorial to national organizations (Canadian Nurses Association, 2003). Within an organization, succession planning progressively engages talented people in major institutional events and offers a structured mentoring so the candidate gains ability and credibility through successful leadership experiences.

According to literature, there are various succession planning models (Abdollahi et al., 2018), such as in Turkey, the nursing professional associations' advisory role conducts the selection process (Kantek & Kavla, 2007). In Australia, the ministry of health participates in selection through active sectors and service areas. In this country, nurses with higher work and management experiences are more likely to be selected as nursing managers. Meanwhile, the Australian nursing and midwifery federation also holds courses to enhance the communication and management skills of nurses (Duffield et al., 2011). In the United Kingdom, governmental and non-governmental organizations outside the national medical system of the country, such as the center for excellence in services and the national institute of health, carry out research on the characteristics of nursing managers and help them meet selection criteria through feedback to service delivery units (McSherry et al., 2012). In the United States, there are various criteria for selecting nursing managers, which are largely in line with UK standards, with the distinction being made on the multidimensional nature of nursing manager services. For example, research and educational experiences are of higher priority. The selection process in US hospitals is based on senior managers' selection of qualified nurses active in the hospital or recruiting advertisements, which determine the demands and expectations of the hospital from the nursing manager (Hart, 2010). Major organizations, such as Johnson & Johnson Company have long-standing programs for nursing executive leadership. The three-week Nurse Executive Fellowships have been held in conjunction with the University of Pennsylvania's Wharton Business School for 25 years. This year's class welcomed the 1000th fellow and attracted nurse leaders from around the United States.

These approaches, however, indicated the various institutions being a part of succession planning. This may describe a political structure or line in the selection process.

Despite various approaches explained above, the COVID-19 has changed the best practices in recruiting nurse managers and has brought succession planning to a new level. What happens if executive nurse managers and middle-line or first-line nurse managers contract the COVID-19? What if they quit? Who is in line to be the next manager? Are the internal people ready? Or will external people need to be hired? This chapter discuss existing problems and steps that the succession planning committee should employ during the crisis. The succession planning program may reduce recruiting expenses, increase leadership continuity, and decrease role-transition stress.

EXISTING PROBLEMS AND RECOMMENDATIONS

Based on our experience, there are several problems in the hospitals as reasons why succession planning is not developed, like the following:

1. The hospitals do not pay attention to potential internal leaders, and mostly they are unprepared for a leadership or managerial position vacancy. In other words, succession planning does not exist. Many nurses are selected to be nurse managers only based on their clinical skills. However, clinical skills and managerial skills are completely different. Nurses who have advanced clinical skills are not guaranteed to become competent managers or leaders. Therefore, it is

recommended for every hospital to develop a succession planning committee to prepare their future leaders.
2. There is no process to assess internal talents due to no available instruments nor sets of managerial or leadership competencies. Managerial and leadership competencies should be updated. We cannot use generic competencies developed 10 or 20 years ago to be applied in the COVID-19 era today. Some competence dimensions may still be practical, such as leadership, conflict management, personnel management, etc., but not technology competencies and communication skills. The nurse managers cannot use telephone calls only to provide telehealth; they also need skills to use computers or apps for a videoconference. Some hospitals have also been developing humanoid robots to provide care, which requires advanced competencies in technology development (Betriana et al., 2020). Besides, communication skills should also be developed considering multi-generations of the staff, such as millennial and alpha generations who prefer to talk instantly and transparently and communicate through apps and social media (Gunawan, 2016).
3. There is no coaching or preceptorship program for potential leaders. This is closely related to point one. When the hospital is ready to develop a succession planning program, the next problem is that there are no coaches and preceptors to provide the program. Not all nurse managers accept to be appointed as a preceptor. Although they have the experience to be a nurse manager, many cannot coach or educate someone to be a leader. Coaching requires other skills, such as mentoring and empowering to make it successful. Besides, budgeting to hire external managers is another issue to resolve. The hospitals should prepare their nurse managers and ensure that they can transfer their knowledge, skills, and attitude to the next generation of managers/leaders.
4. There are unclear career paths and fewer developmental opportunities for staff. If the hospitals do not plan the future career of their employees, indeed the succession planning will never exist. The hospital managers should create a career planning system to ensure that the employees know what they can become in the future, so they are motivated to engage in the development process.

STEPS FOR EFFECTIVE SUCCESSION PLANNING

Every nurse is a candidate to lead (Fray & Sherman, 2017), and therefore, they need to be prepared. Succession planning should have been created even before the COVID-19 pandemic. But it seems the conversation about succession planning during the COVID-19 crisis is becoming a hot topic. Based on the literature review and our lessons learned, we offer steps for effective succession planning.

Step 1: Establishing a Succession Planning Committee

This step aims to establish a committee for contributing to succession planning. This step includes the following questions: (1) *Who are they?* This may consist of hospital boards, nursing board members, nursing associations, professional organizations, governmental or nongovernmental organizations, university faculty; (2) *What are their roles and responsibilities?* This should be clear where the lines of accountability exist; (3) *Is their existence on an ongoing and continuous basis?* It should be stated clearly. It may be updated yearly. However, generally, the succession planning program is a 12- to 36-month process of preparation, not pre-selection; (4) Is the focus of the *succession planning only for selecting top nurse managers, middle-line nurse managers, and/ or first-line or unit nurse managers?* This question should be confirmed because some hospitals only conduct succession planning for unit nurse managers and because the targeted levels will impact the needed curriculum; (5) *What are the steps needed for successful succession planning?* This should be described clearly to prevent an overlapping process.

Step 2: Developing Selection Criteria

Once the succession planning committee is established, the next step is to develop criteria for selecting nurse managers. It may include organizational commitment, work experience, management experiences, research and educational experiences, and managerial and leadership competencies.

Organizational commitment—organizational commitment is essential for identifying internal talent (individuals with high-leadership potential). Organizational commitment refers to the extent to which nurses associate with their organization and its goals (Dinc, 2017) or desire to remain in an organization (Colquitt et al., 2016). HR managers or nursing managers should be able to assess the organizational commitment of internal nurse talent using validated and reliable tools.

Managerial and leadership competencies - it is no secret that the managerial and leadership competencies vary among hospitals, and they are continually updated. Therefore, HR and nursing managers should establish the standard of competence to use for succession planning. The standard should be validated and described clearly with differing sets of competencies for unit managers, middle-line managers, or top managers. Perhaps, the hospitals just use the validated competencies. It is because the hospitals lack resources to develop leadership and managerial competencies. Huston (2008) proposed eight essential leadership competencies for nurse leaders in 2020, including (1) a global perspective on healthcare and professional nursing issues, (2) technology skills, (3) expert decision-making skills based on evidence, (4) ability to create cultures to enhance care quality and patient safety, (5) understanding and intervening in a political process appropriately, (6) collaborative and team-building skills, (7) ability to balance performance expectations and authenticity, and (8) ability to adapt to a healthcare system characterized by rapid change and chaos. Gunawan (2019) developed seven dimensions of managerial competence of first-line nurse managers, including leadership, facilitating spiritual nursing care, self-management, staffing, and professional development, utilizing informatics, financial management, and applying quality care improvement. American Organization of Nurse Executives (2015) developed nurse executive competencies, including communication, knowledge, leadership, professionalism, and business skills.

Work and management experiences—it is no doubt that some hospitals require work and management experience as criteria for selecting nurse managers (Abdollahi et al., 2018). It may be five to ten years of experience to be able to apply for first-line nurse managers; however, some may not require the experience for the selection criteria. Therefore, it should be described clearly.

Research and educational experiences—some hospitals require research and academic experience as the selection criteria of nurse managers (Abdollahi et al., 2018). Generally, a higher position requires a higher educational background. The research experience is seen from their records in academic publications.

Step 3: Developing Methods for Identifying Internal Talents

Next, the succession planning committees identify high-potential internal talent based on the selection criteria, especially based on the organizational commitment and managerial and leadership competencies. HR managers should be working closely with unit managers because they conduct a regular performance appraisal and are more likely to know the staff. Nurses who have a higher score could be interviewed for their career trajectories (Evans, 2016). Sometimes, nurses do not want to jump into a leadership role. This is homework for nurse managers that being a manager is fun and challenging.

Step 4: Identifying and Building the Internal Talent Pool

After the methods for identifying internal talents have been developed, the next step is to identify and build the internal talent pool within a hospital. HR and nursing managers will be in charge of finding the high-potential nurses to be the next leaders' candidates. The agreement between the hospital and the internal talents should be made to confirm that the internal talents will follow the succession planning program until the end.

Step 5: Developing Succession Planning Programs Based on the Need

Once the internal talents have been selected, the committee will develop a succession planning program based on the need of each talent. According to Gardner (1995), leadership development can be done in formal and informal methods. The formal methods include identifying the competencies needed, reviewing the process and content of training to meet the need, considering how to customize the training for specific individual needs, having a follow-up process to reinforce the training, and conducting pre and post-training discussions with the 'rising stars.' While the informal methods are coached by a leader, including sharing experience to improve in specific areas, modeling the behavior, clarifying the positive and negative consequences of behavior, providing the big picture on how the specific behavior has a global impact, and using confidence building.

Byham (2002) developed the acceleration pool system that provides an accurate assessment of development needs and an environment to acquire the desirable leadership competencies. In this pool system, the candidates will have an assigned mentor, receive feedback, coaching, training, and opportunities to attend board or committee development sessions, attend the strategic planning association, co-chair a committee or a workgroup, chair conference sessions and participate in focus groups among experts. In this program, the candidates will get information related to organizational knowledge, position challenges, competencies, and leadership derailers. The staff leaders will also place the candidates into situations where they can experience the real challenge and develop competencies. Example: Some institutions require each candidate to complete an improvement project as a component of the program. The project planning process exposes the candidate to organizational issues, guiding the use of resources to achieve a major goal for the organization, and orchestrating communication of change in a way that champions the needed outcomes. Finally, monitoring the change to assure assimilation of the improvement completes the project.

Based on our experience, the program should place the candidates as a team leader in the nursing unit and an assistant of the front managers if they are meant to be groomed as a first-line nurse manager. In this program, the candidates will plan nursing care for all nursing staff in the unit and conduct or observe bedside nursing care under the supervision of the front managers. The team leader and the front managers work collaboratively to conduct staffing, financial management, and other competencies. In this program, the candidates will be observed and coached in an actual situation. The outcome in this program is about commitment and competence and the quality of care, staff nurses' outcomes and satisfaction (including quality of life), and patients' outcomes and satisfaction.

Step 6: Implementing the Succession Planning Process

The implementation of the succession planning process varies among organizations. It can be one to three years, dependent on the assessments and the needs. In an urgent situation, such as during the COVID-19 pandemic, in which, for instance, one of the nursing managers contracts the virus, the succession planning committee should decide who will replace the position from the internal talents, based on the latest assessment of organizational commitment and managerial or leadership competencies. Therefore, the evaluation should be done routinely every six months or at least yearly. If the urgent needs exist before six months, the hospitals may need to invite the other nursing managers from outside hospitals, but they are under the same company or the same owner. Some hospitals may ask other managers from different ownership. It depends on each hospital's policy. However, the success of the succession planning process is assessed based on the competence and commitment of the candidates as well as the nursing and patient outcomes.

Step 7: Making Selections from the Talent Pool

After all processes have been implemented, the succession planning committees will make selections from the talent pool to fill needed positions.

EXAMPLES OF SUCCESSION PLANNING IN A HOSPITAL CONTEXT

In Thailand, succession planning should be created prior to the selection of a head nurse or nurse manager. The succession planning committees include the nurse director, vice nurse director, head nurses of inpatient and outpatient units, and academic leaders or nurse educators.

The following criteria to be a head nurse or nurse manager include (1) Having a master's degree in nursing administration and one special certificate (based on each ward/unit), and (2) at least an RN with level 8. This opportunity is open for every nurse, not only nurses inside hospitals but also nurses outside hospitals.

Once the internal talents have been selected, the succession planning committees set the program, most likely for one year:

- The candidates are required to do a presentation in front of hospital managers and nurse managers about vision and mission, leadership, and management experiences.
- An interview will also take place.
- The committees will set a project assignment or pre-manager program coached by head nurses or certified persons.
- Some hospitals provide a short course for four months focusing on leadership and management and a field trip study or benchmark to another hospital or another department.

- The probationary period for three months in a planned position and department.
- Last, all candidates will be evaluated by the succession planning committees, head nurses, peers, and staff. All the results will be announced.

It is noteworthy that the succession planning program in each hospital in Thailand may vary. There is no universal agreement in conducting the program or selecting the candidates. Issues related to nepotism, bureaucracy, and political bargaining may exist and must be addressed.

In Indonesia, not all hospitals apply a succession planning program to select nurse managers. Approaches to recruit and select nurse managers vary among public hospitals: (1) it depends on the availability of nurses who a hold higher education. Those who have a higher education and longer time in the field (senior nurses) are selected first, with or without assessing the competence but based on the performance every month; (2) every nurse has a chance to be a nurse manager (first-line nurse manager) if they have at least three years for nurses who hold a bachelor degree, and five years for nurses with a diploma degree, with or without assessing competence (based on the function of career ladder system in each hospital); and (3) bureaucracy is sometimes involved during recruitment and selection of nurse managers (Basyaruddin, 2018; Hermini, 2018; Indonesian Nurse Managers Association, 2016a; Saputra, 2018). However, an interview by the head of nursing departments is used to select all nurse managers (Basyaruddin, 2018; Hermini, 2018; Nazliansyah, 2019; Saputra, 2018).

The career ladder for a nurse manager is a part of the nursing career ladder system in general in a hospital, which describes the direction of the career path of nurse managers into five levels (nurse manager 1–5) and three categories (low, middle, and top managers) (Indonesian Nurse Managers Association, 2016b) (Table 8.1). However, the career path among public hospitals varies. Some public hospitals apply this path, and some use a different approach. This occurs because the career path by Indonesian National Nurse Managers Association has not yet become the nursing standard in Indonesia (Basyaruddin, 2018; Hermini, 2018; Nazliansyah, 2019; Saputra, 2018).

The required educational level to be the first-line nurse managers is a minimum Diploma III and IV with clinical experience of five years, or Bachelor level with clinical experience of three years (Ministry of

Table 8.1 Career path of nurse managers in Indonesia

Nurse manager 1	First-line nurse managers	Low managers
Nurse manager 2	Area managers	Middle managers
Nurse manager 3	Head of sub-nursing department	
Nurse manager 4	Head of nursing department	Top managers
Nurse manager 5	Director/vice director of nursing	

Health, 2017). Some hospitals require at least five years of being a primary nurse, attending management training, and having certification from the Indonesian Nurse Managers Association and Indonesian National Nurses Association (Indonesian Nurse Managers Association, 2016b). While at some hospitals, for being Nurse Manager 1–5, a Hospital Director will directly choose the ones. So, if the director is changed, nurse managers are also changed. It indicates that politics and bureaucracies are involved. Therefore, it is suggested that competence-based selection/succession planning should be fully implemented.

Conclusion

Succession planning must exist to prepare the young generation to be the leaders of tomorrow. Mentorship is the key to succession planning, and it should be well planned. The hospitals should pay attention to the issues related to barriers to the succession planning process and follow each step for leadership development. The clock is ticking; HR and nursing managers must work closely to begin the succession planning program as soon as possible to face the new normal era.

References

Abdollahi, A., Tabibi, J., & Komeili, A. (2018). Selection, recruitment and training of nursing managers in hospitals: A comparative study. *Modern Care Journal*, 15(3). https://doi.org/10.5812/modernc.81682

American Organization of Nurse Executives. (2015). *AONE nurse executive competencies*. American Organization of Nurse Executives. Chicago. Retrieved from https://www.aonl.org/sites/default/files/aone/nec.pdf

Basyaruddin, E. (2018). [Personal communication - A first-line nurse manager at a public hospital].

Betriana, F., Tanioka, T., Locsin, R., Malini, H., & Lenggogeni, D. P. (2020). Are Indonesian nurses ready for healthcare robots during the COVID-19 pandemic? *Belitung Nursing Journal*, 6(3), 63–66. https://doi.org/10.33546/bnj.1114

Byham, W. C. (2002). A new look at succession management. *Ivey Business Journal*, 66(5), 10–12.

Canadian Nurses Association. (2003). *Succession planning for nursing leadership*. Retrieved from https://www.cna-aiic.ca/~/media/cna/page-content/pdf-en/succession-planning-for-nursing-leadership.pdf?la=en

Colquitt, J. A., LePine, J. A., & Wesson, M. J. (2016). *Organizational behavior: Improving performance and commitment in the workplace* (5th ed.). McGraw-Hill Education.

Dinc, M. S. (2017). *Organizational behavior in higher education*. Lap Lambert Academic Publishing.

Duffield, C. M., Roche, M. A., Blay, N., & Stasa, H. (2011). Nursing unit managers, staff retention and the work environment. *Journal of Clinical Nursing*, 20(1–2), 23–33.

Evans, J. L. T. (2016). Three first steps for effective succession planning. *American Nurse Today*, 11(9), 36–40.

Fray, B., & Sherman, R. O. (2017). Best practices for nurse leaders: Succession planning. *Professional Case Management*, 22(2), 88–94. https://doi.org/10.1097/ncm.0000000000000214

Gardner, H. (1995). *Leading kinds—An anatomy of leadership*. Basic Books.

Gunawan, J. (2016). Generation Y nurse: What do I need on the workplace? *Belitung Nursing Journal*, 2(3), 44–46. https://doi.org/10.33546/bnj.21

Gunawan, J. (2019). "This is 2019! But I still need to work double shifts and have multiple jobs to keep me alive": A phenomenon among nurses in Indonesia. *Belitung Nursing Journal*, 5(3), 108–110. https://doi.org/10.33546/bnj.810

Hart, M. D. (2010). A Delphi study to determine baseline informatics competencies for nurse managers. *CIN: Computers, Informatics, Nursing*, 28(6), 364–370. https://doi.org/10.1097/ncn.0b013e3181f69d89

Hermini, S. Y. (2018). [Personal communication - A first-line nurse manager at a public hospital].

Huston, C. (2008). Preparing nurse leaders for 2020. *Journal of Nursing Management*, 16(8), 905–911. https://doi.org/10.1111/j.1365-2834.2008.00942.x

Indonesian Nurse Managers Association. (2016a). *Draft of career ladder system of Indonesian nurse managers*. Jakarta: Indonesian Nurse Managers Association.

Indonesian Nurse Managers Association. (2016b). *Nursing ward management in H. Adam Malik hospital*. Retrieved from http://rsham.co.id/wp-content/uploads/2016/02/Manajemen-Ruang-Rawat-_agustus_-2016.pdf

Kantek, F., & Kavla, I. (2007). Nurse-nurse manager conflict: How do nurse managers manage it? *The Health Care Manager, 26*(2), 147–151. https://doi.org/10.1097/01.hcm.0000268618.33491.84

Lotich, P. (2017). *6 tips for creating an effective succession plan*. Retrieved from https://thethrivingsmallbusiness.com/what-is-succession-planning/

McSherry, R., Pearce, P., Grimwood, K., & McSherry, W. (2012). The pivotal role of nurse managers, leaders and educators in enabling excellence in nursing care. *Journal of Nursing Management, 20*(1), 7–19. https://doi.org/10.1111/j.1365-2834.2011.01349.x

Menaldo, V. (2016). *The institutions curse: Natural resources, politics, and development*. Cambridge University Press.

Ministry of Health. (2017). *Regulation of the Ministry of Health of the Republic of Indonesia no 40 year 2017 about development of professional career ladder of clinical nurses*. Ministry of Health, the Republic of Indonesia.

Nazliansyah, N. (2019). [Personal communication—A first-line nurse manager at a public hospital].

Saputra, F. (2018). [Personal communication].

Titzer, J. L., Shirey, M. R., & Hauck, S. (2014). A nurse manager succession planning model with associated empirical outcomes. *JONA: The Journal of Nursing Administration, 44*(1), 37–46. https://doi.org/10.1097/nna.0000000000000019

Index

A
acute respiratory infections (ARIs), 54
adaptability, 42
advance practice nurse (APN), 85
Agile HR, 10
aging population, 32
attendance, 52
authority, 6

B
Babbage, Charles, 4
baby boom generation, 32
best-fit approach, 21
best practice approach, 20
bias, 2
bullying at work, 39
bureaucracy, 2, 90
burnout, 2

C
Cambodia, 2
career, 81
career advancement, 82
career ladder, 102
career paths, 83
career planning and development, 82
centralized CBHRM, 20
civil servants, 43
clinical nurse, 84
coaching, 17, 96
commitment, 39
compassion, 42
compensation, 2
competence, 9, 34
competence-based HRM, 17
competence-based human resource management, 4
competence-based interview, 40
competency, 9
conflict management, 96
Continuous Professional Development (CPD), 87
core competencies, 16
COVID-19, 2, 39, 46, 50, 59, 65, 72, 82
COVID-19 pandemic, 31

D
decentralized CBHRM, 20
discrimination, 38

E
eight-hour day movement, 3
e-learning, 54
Elton Mayo, George, 7
employee referrals, 33
equity, 6
evolution, 3
experiential reward, 64

F
fair, 33
fair pay, 62
fatigue, 82
Fayol, Henri, 5
Fayolism, 5
function, 16

G
games, 58
generations, 2
graduate recruitment, 34

H
harmony, 2
Harvard Analytic Framework, 17
Harvard model, 18
Hawthorne effect, 7
head nurse, 102
Herzberg, Frederick, 9
hospital, 1
human relation movement, 7
human resource management, 9
human resource managers, 33
human resources, 1

I
Indonesia, 45
industrial revolution, 3
infection prevention, 42
infection prevention and control (IPC), 53
instant reward, 63
intangible rewards, 63
intend to leave, 32
intend to quit, 32
interviews, 44

J
job rotations, 34
job security, 39

K
key performance indicator (KPI), 71
knowledge management, 17

L
leadership, 39

M
managerial skills, 95
Maslow, Abraham, 7
matching model, 18
McClelland, David Clarence, 8
McGregor, Douglas, 7
mental health management program, 53
mentorship, 38
Modern Competency Movement, 9
monetary rewards, 64
motivation-hygiene theory, 8

N
need theory, 8

new normal, 46
new normal era, 45, 67, 70
new normal training, 53
non-monetary rewards, 66
nurse migration, 82
nurse residency program, 55
nurses, 1, 72, 84
nurse turnover, 61
nursing, 2
nursing administration, 101
nursing audit, 72
nursing image, 39
nursing leaders, 94
nursing shortage, 31, 82
nursing workforce, 32

O
online lectures, 54
on-the-job training, 55
organizational culture, 58
outcomes, 22
Owen, Robert, 3

P
partnership, 39
patient satisfaction, 72
pay equity, 63
performance, 7
performance appraisal, 72
performance evaluation, 73
performance review, 74
personal protective equipment (PPE), 53
personnel management, 3
Philippines, 82
preceptorship, 96
process, 21
pull factors, 82
push factors, 82

Q
quality care, 1
quality of work-life, 39

R
rating scale method, 71
recognition, 66
recruitment, 36
recruitment and selection, 33
registered nurse, 44
remuneration, 6, 64, 65
retention, 39
rewards and benefits, 61
Routine to Research (R2R), 55

S
scholarship, 43
scientific management, 4
selection, 36
seniority, 76, 90
short course training, 51
skill mix, 39
Smith, Adam, 3
steps for training, 52
stigma, 32
strategic human resource management, 10
stress, 2
structure, 21
succession planning, 94

T
talent management, 10
Taylor, Frederic Winslow, 4
Taylorism, 4
technological performance appraisal, 72
technological skills, 42
telehealth, 42
Thailand, 42, 85

Theory X & Y, 7
total quality management (TQM), 10
traditional HRM, 19
training and development, 51
transformation, 2
transparency, 38
transparent pay, 67
turnover, 2

V
ventilator management, 53
Vietnam, 2
violence, 32

W
World Health Organization (WHO), 82

The manufacturer's authorised representative in the EU is Springer Nature Customer Service Centre GmbH, Europaplatz 3, 69115 Heidelberg, Germany. If you have any concerns regarding our products, please contact ProductSafety@springernature.com

Printed and bound by CPI Group (UK) Ltd, Croydon, CR0 4YY

25/03/2026

02078205-0004